WARNHAM.

Ron A.H. Muggeridge
1983

*Molly at the opening meet of the
Crawley and Horsham Foxhounds at Knepp Castle*

Molly

The Years at Ends Place

Molly

The Years at Ends Place

by R.A.H. Muggeridge

SMH BOOKS

British Library Cataloguing in Publication Data

A catalogue record for this book is available from the
British Library

ISBN hardback 0 9512619 4 0

First published December 1993 by
SMH BOOKS
Pear Tree Cottage, Watersfield, PULBOROUGH
West Sussex, RH20 lNG

Typeset by
INKWELL, Cocking, West Sussex

Printed and bound in Great Britain by
Hillman Printers (Frome) Ltd

for Charles, Mark and Nicola

Molly with Jack Clarke

CONTENTS

ACKNOWLEDGEMENTS

I should like to thank the following, for their help in the preparation of this book:

Capt. R.A. (Sandy) Villiers

Mrs. Pamela Davey

Mrs. Joyce Driver

Mrs. Marjorie Leslie

Mr Johnny Foran

Mrs. Muriel Dann (née Trask)

Mr. George Tusler

Mrs. Doris Downer

Mrs. Rose Musgrave

Mr. Robert Muggeridge

and

Mrs. Sheila Barratt.

Finally, I am especially grateful to Mr. G.G.A. Gregson, who has helped so substantially to bring this book into being.

R.A.H.M.

FOREWORD

This history of the Gregson family covers the long period - 1908 to 1985 - when they were resident owners of Ends Place, Warnham, in Sussex.

Dividing up those years according to the number during which members of the family lived at Ends Place, it soon becomes apparent that Molly Gregson's time there far exceeds that of the others. Consequently, the story revolves mainly around her life, and those of her parents, her husband Harry, her children and grandchildren, and other relatives.

Molly Gregson was born into a wealthy family who owned a prosperous West Country cloth mill. A lively young girl, who started riding at a very early age, she married at nineteen and, by the time she was twenty-one, had had two children. Soon after her marriage, because her husband travelled frequently and was away for long periods every year, she was faced with the task of running the large household at Ends Place*. Because of her background, being fully conversant with business affairs and the employment and management of staff, she proved herself to be undaunted by this task.

Indeed, Molly was a forceful character, held in awe by her staff, both inside and outside the house. Yet she was greatly admired and respected , and this became more evident as the years went by, and she came to be one of the largest landowners in that part of Sussex. Even in her latter years, she went on running the estate, ably assisted by her staff. She continued to live at Ends Place until her death.

---

* *at one time known as Endes Place*

To the end, Molly retained her interest in hunting, horses, hounds and farming. In her ninetieth year, she attended the Alfriston Agricultural Show, where Cecil Young had once trained horses for her husband.

INTRODUCTION

When Charles Bulpin purchased Ends Place in 1908, it was in a very poor state of repair, and he immediately started the work of restoring and rebuilding.

In 1830, a serious fire had destroyed much of the house. The fire is said to have been caused by a faulty flue in the laundry which set one of the beams alight. This necessitated the reconstruction of the main part of the house.

From various documents and old letters, it is possible to piece together some of the early history of Ends Place. There has been much speculation and guesswork on this subject through the years, but little has been discovered prior to 1800.

In my book *Warnham : A History*, I included an article on Ends Place. I have drawn on this, but have updated it with facts and suggestions which have come to light since that book's publication in 1985.

Even up to 1907, Ends Place had often been described as a great rambling place. During the whole of its existence, it was intended to be self-supporting, having amenities along the lines of those found in small villages. There were wheelwrights, blacksmiths, carpenters, shops, kennels for foxhounds, stables for horses, outhouses for cattle, sheep, pigs; and there was accommodation for grooms and huntsmen. There were indoor staff and it is known that at one time a grandmother, with the help of maids and a weaver, spun the flax grown on the estate. All these employees were kept at Charles Bulpin Gregson's expense.

The size of this small, industrious settlement can be judged by the written record of an elderly lady. In 1908, she noted that five or six sheep were killed weekly with, occasionally, a bullock, and pigs, poultry and geese, all for house consumption. She also mentions that the young people of the house always had their own apartments, even after leaving school.

In a letter to a certain 'Clara', also written in 1908, it seems fairly certain that the lady whose writings I have quoted, and will continue to quote, was 'Aunt Emmie', the great granddaughter of Matthew and Sarah Napper, resident at Ends Place from 1746 to 1801.

However, long before that, 'Aunt Emmie' records, a Mr. Gibbons told her that there was a 'Knight of the Golden Spurs' living at Ends Place. (The Battle of Golden Spurs took place in Flanders in 1302.) If this is true, and it is difficult to confirm due to the turbulence of those years, it would seem that Ends Place existed two hundred years before Warnham Church was dedicated to the Blessed Virgin Mary as an Anglican Church (in or before 1505).

Early records show that the land surrounding Ends Place came under the Manor of Slaughterford, together with land round Warnham Mill and Warnham Place. It was all owned by the Yates, or Yeats family going back to 1639 and before that, the Youngers were the owners, from 1616.

The next bit of history is seventeenth-century. In the mid-1980s, part of a wall and pillar fell down, from the gateway to what was then known as Hall Court. In the foundations of the pillar were found a silver spoon, and a gold posy ring bearing the inscription 'The gift of a faithful frend' (sic). The ring could only have been worn by someone with a tiny finger. The spoon bore the date 1666 - the year of the Great Fire of London.

Dandy (or Dendy) Napper, the son of Matthew and Sarah Napper (who are commemorated in Warnham Church) was born in 1880. He married Mary Knight, of Stamerham. He was known to be a great spendthrift and when he died in

1820, a considerable part of Ends Place property had to be sold, to pay off his debts and make provision for his widow and younger children.

Either of Dandy Napper's brothers, John (born in 1780) or Frederick, could have been Emmie's father or uncle.

After Dandy Napper's death, his eldest son, Henry, continued to live at Old House (the name by which Ends Place was often referred to), until it was burnt down.

According to the 1840 Title awards, a Richard Clemson Barnett then owned Ends Place, Charmans, Betchetts, Cradles, West House (possibly Westbrook), Benland and Maltmayes. Separate reference is in fact made to Old House, which could have been confused with Byfleets Farm or Hill House. Although owned by Richard Clemson Barnett, Ends Place was at that time occupied by Mr. Francis Wells, as recorded in the 1841 to 1855 Census. He moved to Cradles Lodge (now Rowhook Manor) in 1855. Mr. William Churchman moved to Ends Place in 1858 and live there until about 1905. His landlord was Mr. A.W. Owen, of the Old Palace, Richmond. It was from Mr. Owen that Charles Bulpin Gregson bought the estate.

In those days, 'Aunt Emmie' remembered, a long drive led out to the public road. On one side of the drive, there were about five ponds before the main gate, the two pillars of which were each topped with an enormous globe.*

With so much building work needing to be done at Ends Place, it was probably more convenient for Charles

---

The gate and globes are thought to be those which were partially destroyed by a tank or armoured vehicle, in World War II. (Such vehicles were often seen in and around the estate at that time.) The damaged gates, after lying for a long time beside the drive, were eventually bought by Mr. Ken Prichard Jones in 1985, to be repaired and erected at his own drive entrance at Field Place, Warnham.

Bulpin and his wife to continue to live in India, where they had spent so many of their earlier years (although communication with home caused difficulties).

Except for a small section to the rear of the house, almost the entire building was changed.

Having lived long in India, Charles Bulpin must have grown tired of so much heat, and that could be why the new house was designed so that the main living quarters and bedrooms faced north. They looked out on to the drive, fine lawns, the entrance to the Beasleys and the ponds. Later, tennis courts and a cricket area were added on the north side.

Once the new house had been completed, Mrs. Gregson lived for most of the time at Ends Place, but Charles Bulpin continued to spend much of his time in India on business.

The Gregsons had two children : Henry George, who was born in 1894 and Margaret, born in 1896.

Chapter 1

Eric Alexander Mackay
Molly's Uncle

Probably the best known member of the family was Eric Alexander Mackay - 'Major Eric', as he was always called. He was the elder son of Mr. and Mrs. Alexander Mackay, of Holt Manor and later, of The Grange, Trowbridge. Alexander Mackay's family originated in a little village called Dunbeath, in Caithness, Scotland. In 1860, they moved down to Trowbridge, where Alexander took up a post in the cloth mills, later to become Palmer and Mackay Limited.

He was educated at Cheam and Eton. He had three children. A pillar of the church, he frequently entertained the Bishops of Bath and Salisbury.

He was a great historian and, at The Grange, had a marvellous collection of books, manuscripts, documents such as the Charter of Devizes, and six volumes in manuscript of *Wiltshire* by Aubrey and Jackson. The whole house was steeped in history and historical objects, like the desk formerly owned by John Ruskin and the signatures of, and letters written by many famous people of the day. There were oils and watercolours, including family portraits, by well known artists, particularly W. Birket Forster.

Major Eric followed his father into Trowbridge mill in 1898. Apart from several years' absence on military service, he took an active part in the business and, from 1919 to 1952, was joint managing director.

In 1898, he joined the 1st Wilts Rifle Volunteers as a

Second Lieutenant and in 1908, became one of the original
members of the Territorial Army Association, holding a
commissioned rank in the 4th Battalion, the Wiltshire
Regiment. He was mobilised in 1914, and sailed for India.
There, he served with the battalion in Delhi until April, 1915,
when he was made Staff Captain. In 1917, he embarked for
service in Egypt and Palestine, and he was badly wounded at
the Battle of El Mesmiyeh, while fighting the Turks. He
recovered, however, and after the war, he returned to
England, where he continued to serve in the Wiltshire
Territorial Army Association.

In the Second World War, Eric took over the duties of
secretary of the T.A.A. and he became a member of the
newly formed Wiltshire Territorial and Auxiliary Forces
Association. He was also Commanding Officer of the
Trowbridge Home Guard during the Second World War.

He was the author of *The History of the Wiltshire
Home Guard* (1947). Proceeds from the sale of this went to
the Old Comrades Association.

He always took a great interest in the British Legion
and, distinguished by his fine bearing, would lead the parades
to the church and to the War Memorial on Remembrance
Sunday. On Open Days, he held military band concerts on
the lawns of The Grange.

All his life, he was very active. As Master of the
Trowbridge Beagles, he turned out in all weathers to hunt.
An expert fisherman (unsurpassed at eighty, in the year of his
death), he was often to be seen on his beat on the Wylye.

He was a deeply religious man, and regularly
worshipped at St. James's Parish Church, Trowbridge.
Described as a man of great moral courage - as soldier,
magistrate, industrialist and sportsman, he had a great sense
of duty. He showed great kindness and tenderness to people,

and would go out of his way to help those in trouble. Children loved him and would rush up to meet him. He was heard to say: "I feel so honoured when they do this". Every Christmas, for forty-two years, he sent a present and a card to his old Indian servant.

A Grand Master Mason and trustee of various societies, he was a staunch Tory in politics (most of the West Country was Liberal at the time) and was always active in the Party.

For seven years, until 1955, he was Chairman of Trowbridge Magistrates. In 1958, he survived a severe illness and operation. After a period of convalescence, he resumed an active part in running the mills. However, following a later relapse in health, he died in 1961, at his home in Hilperton Village.

Hundreds of people from all over the country attended Major Eric's funeral at St. James's, Trowbridge. Covered with the family tartan, the coffin was followed by the standards of Trowbridge British Legion, which were dipped as 'The Last Post' was sounded. After cremation at Bath, his ashes were interred at Hilperton.

Chapter 2

George Eric Mackay
Molly's Father

Born in 1872, George Eric Mackay was the second son of Mr. and Mrs. Alexander Mackay. Like his brother, he was educated at Cheam, Eton and Jesus College, Cambridge. At Eton, he won his Upper Sixpenny colours for cricket and for many years he played for the Eton Ramblers and the Wiltshire Wanderers.

After leaving university, where he read law, he was commissioned in the Royal Wiltshire Yeomanry, and served in the Rood Ashton troop. He reached the rank of Major in 1906 and served throughout the First World War at their headquarters in Chippenham, in liaison with the American troops there. During this time, he was attached to the North Irish Horse.

In 1895, he married Katie, daughter of Mr. and Mrs. Nicolson Browne, of Chiseldon. They had two daughters, Molly and Jean.

Miss Kitty Browne   Mr. G. E. MacKay

CHISLEDON.
*MARRIAGE OF MISS BROWNE
AND MR. MACKAY.*
A PRETTY WEDDING.

Social life is not so eventful in the quiet but pretty village of Chiseldon, now in all its summer beauty, and therefore the interesting wedding which took place at the old parish church on Wednesday last was looked forward to with much pleasure, and something more than local interest attached to the event. If there be any truth in the old adage "happy is the bride whom the sun shines on ," then the eldest daughter of Mr W. E. Nicolson Browne, ought to be happy indeed, for the brightest sunshine prevailed throughout the day. The wedding was that of Miss Katie, daughter of Mr W. E. N. Browne, of The Cottage, Chiseldon, to George Eric, eldest son of Mr Alexander Mackay, J.P., of The Grange, Trowbridge. Mr Browne and his family are so well known in social circles, and the bride is so appreciated in the village in her associations with various parochial agencies, that it was not surprising to see the whole village *en fête* for the occasion, and visitors present from all the adjoining villages and from the town of Swindon. Everywhere in the village were to be seen signs of good wishes for the bride and bridegroom's happiness and prosperity. Near the railway station were two floral arches - one erected by Mr E. J. Sheppard, and bearing the wish "Welcome;" and another, the tasteful work of Mr T. Mead and Mr Jesse Palmer, bearing he words "Long life and happiness" and "Success to the bride and bridegroom." The church too, was beautifully decorated with the choicest of flowers and evergreens by Mrs Cally and Mrs Walker; whilst in the chancel were nicely arranged a lovely lot of hot-house plants, kindly lent by Mr Davy, of Burderop Park, and Mr Butler, of Chisledon House. The scene in the interior of the church was rendered all the more pleasant and attractive by reason of the charming dresses of the ladies present - and they were not a few.

The ceremony was fixed for two o'clock, and long before the hour the church was crowded to excess, and the route from Chisledon Cottage to the church was also studded with spectators. The officiating clergy were the Rev. Canon Fleming, vicar of St. Michael's, Chester Square, London, and the Rev. J. H. Calley, vicar of Chisledon. Soon after they had taken up their positions at the chancel steps, the bride arrived and entered the church leaning on the arm of her father, who gave her away. She was charmingly attired in a lovely dress of ivory satin, trimmed with point d'Alençon lace; she also wore a wreath of real orange blossoms and a tulle veil, fastened with a diamond swallow ornament, the gift of the bridegroom. She carried a beautiful shower bouquet of white roses and carnations, also the gift of the bridegroom. The six bridesmaids were Miss Phyllis Browne and Miss Christabel Browne (sisters of the bride), Miss Alice Mackay (sister of the bridegroom), Miss Edith Hill (cousin of the bridegroom), Miss Dorothy Bagley and Miss Joan Bagley (cousins of the bride). They were each attired in beautifully made dresses of white silk, trimmed with ecru insertion and blue ribbons over blue satin. Each wore Marie Antoinette picture hats of Raffia straw, trimmed with pale blue ribbons and pink roses (supplied by Mademoiselle Adine, of Severn Stoke, Worcester) ; they also wore bronze shoes and white kid gloves, with gold and pearl bangles, and each carried a bouquet of pink roses tied with white ribbons, presented by the bridegroom.

May 29th 1895

With his wife, he was a follower of the Beaufort Hunt all his life. In his day, he was a good shot and a fine fisherman.

For nineteen years, from 1919, Major Mackay was a director of Palmer and Mackay.

He died in 1944 (his wife had pre-deceased him in 1930), after a long, painful illness. During his last six years, he had been unable to take part in the sports he loved, or enjoy the delights of country life, to which he was devoted. The Duke of Beaufort brought hounds to his window, in order that he might see them one last time. While ill, he was tended with unfailing and loving care by his gardener, Tucker, and Nurse Coffey, who earned the family's deep gratitude for doing so.

Chapter 3

Charles Bulpin Gregson
Harry's Father

Charles Bulpin Gregson was the son of a prosperous shipping family in Liverpool, where there were many Gregsons.

A stockbroker and qualified Solicitor, he went out to work in India with Andrew Yule, a branch of the East India Company, and became a successful businessman in the last years of the nineteenth century, setting up his own stockbroking company, Reed Ward, and forming private investment companies, registered in Calcutta, in which all the shares were held by the Gregson family. These were the Warnham Company Limited, Sussex Company Limited, Winkfield Company Limited, Windsor Company Limited, and Berkshire Company Limited. Charles Bulpin also owned a tin mine in Burma, and extensive property in India, including a lodge at Dalma Hills, close to Jamshedpore (now Tatas).

Later, a very old man at Reed Ward said that 'Mr. Charles', as he was always known, "could smell a rupee in another man's pocket".*

The family home was a large Georgian house and gardens at 24 Park Street, Calcutta.** The two children of

---

* *This was told to Geoffrey, on his first visit to Calcutta.*

** *When Geoffrey saw it in 1958, the house had been turned into a war hospital. Later, it was converted into a permanent hospital, the gardens turned into closed-in wards for the patients. It is still a hospital, frequently visited by Mother Teresa.*

24 Park Street in Calcutta, in December 1921

Charles Bulpin's marriage to Annie Caroline were both born at Park Street. Extensive outside and inside staff were employed on the property.

Charles was the leading racehorse owner in Calcutta, owned bloodstock, raced thoroughbreds, and hunted regularly in Southern India. He owned a silver-topped measuring stick, given to him by his trainer, G. Mills, dated 1893. However, being tall and of heavy build, it is unlikely that he ever race rode. He did participate in another popular sport of the day in Delhi: hunting wild pig.

Charles Bulpin bought Ends Place, which included the main house, farm, land, and cottages, for £12,000. Considerable negotiation went on between the seller and purchaser before the deal was struck. Mr. A. W. Owen wanted to leave behind his sheep, cattle and some furniture, until he was able to move them, agreeing to pay for their keep and storage. Charles, however, very much the businessman, wanted the house, barns, stables and other buildings cleared before settlement.

One amusing incident which arose from these stipulations was that, after purchase had been made, Charles claimed fifteen shillings from the seller, because two swans mentioned in the valuation had flown from the drive ponds.

Completion of the settlement was lengthy and at one stage Mr. Owen sent a letter, through his Solicitor, requesting urgent action. The delay was no doubt caused by Charles being in India.

At the beginning of the twentieth century, England was undergoing great changes. Steam power had replaced the use of horses on the land, with the consequent loss of employment. The First World War brought its own problems, and in the 1920s work of any kind was difficult to obtain, since the country was going through a recession.

Even for those in work, times were hard. The worker was being exploited. Conditions of employment were deplorable, particularly in the factories and on the railways. Those in agriculture were finding fewer jobs available, as often farmers found it more economical to let their land lie idle. Workers were having to endure the increasing hardships of low wages, longer hours, and no pay, if absent - whatever the reason. Few, if any, families had means of support in times of illness. There was no such thing as sickness benefit. A few charities did exist, but many in need of their help were too proud to ask for it. It was considered unacceptable to be without work, and to ask for charity. Friends or neighbours (who might after all find themselves one day in similar circumstances) did often help.

Offering tied accommodation meant of course that employers were able to exert strong control, over their workers. On average, the rent charged was about four shillings (4/-), that is, about 20p a week: a ridiculous sum, one might think, but it has to be considered in the context of what an employee might receive for a week's work. He might receive eighteen shillings (about £1) a week, and with that he had to provide for a family of four, six, or more. The wife could earn about two shillings (10p) a day, for eight hours' work in the fields.

Live-in housemaids earned £4 to £12 a year, cooks, £20, ladies' maids, £16.

However, for those in tied accommodation or with live-in jobs, there was always the threat of dismissal, and the possibility that they would have to vacate their rooms or cottages.

Of the main employers in the Warnham area, the Gregsons appear to have been the most popular, and there is no evidence of their having evicted any employee from tied accommodation, although other landowners in the vicinity were constantly vying with each other to buy properties that became available through eviction.

This concern for their staff is no doubt the reason why the Gregsons were the favourite employers. All staff had uniforms provided and could expect an average one day off per month, plus an occasional free evening. Some perks were available to outside workers, such as vegetables, eggs, milk and sometimes, a rabbit.

Chapter 4

The Changing Times

For a century before the Gregsons came to Ends Place, many changes had already taken place that were to affect the agricultural estates. To understand fully the impact of those changes, it will be helpful to summarise events during that period of history.

The greatest development was the Industrial Revolution, which affected not only England but the whole world.

In Britain, workers were leaving the land in massive numbers to enter the better-paid iron and steel industries. While benefiting from easier to obtain and, for many, better accommodation in the industrial areas developed specifically to house them, the country people found working conditions less healthy than those of the outdoor life to which they had been accustomed. The extreme heat from furnaces and boilers, together with the dust, oil, smoke and fumes gradually proved to be a great danger to health. Working hours, moreover, were less convenient, since they involved shiftwork. This, and the long hours, would often deprive the workers of much needed weekend leisure activities and time for relaxation.

With the transition from one way of life to another, changes were also taking place in the realm of transport. This was to change the lifestyle of thousands, for most of whom there was no alternative.

The increasing use of steam led to the opening of many

new roads, which gave access to the fast growing network of railways. Steam rollers and steam engines provided the means of transporting heavy loads. This of course reduced the number of horses required, making fewer opportunities for carters, coachmen and those in allied occupations. The introduction of steam to supplement or replace the horse for agricultural work meant, as we have already seen, that fewer workers were required.

The steam engine, with pulling power so much greater than that of horses, was replacing the animals in work for which a team of them had previously been required. The steam engine was also ideal for transporting trees on the running gear. More and more steam was being used for driving machines such as saw mills and threshers, the movement of fun fairs, and the generation of electricity for lighting. Some of the steam engines were magnificently decorated. (Many of these can be seen still today at rallies all over the country, kept in perfect working order.)

During this industrial transformation, the motor car was replacing the horse carriage for the wealthy. Horse buses, which had been a familiar sight in towns and cities in the first quarter of the twentieth century, were also on the decline in favour of mechanical transport. The transitional period created considerable congestion and hazards, with a great number of accidents. The horse droppings themselves were a danger, particularly in bad weather. The hordes of sweepers continually required to sweep and shovel away dung, in the wake of horse traffic, themselves increased the risk of accidents.

And this was when Charles Bulpin Gregson came to Sussex.

An interesting point regarding the rights to properties, right up to and into the twentieth century, was that although land acreage was registered, actual boundaries were often vague. Thus, having purchased Ends Place, Charles Bulpin had to walk right along the boundaries of his land, leaving marks on trees, footpaths, and wherever else convenient.

To walk the original estate, thought to be about 1,000 acres, he could have started at the lodge at the Warnham Village end of the drive, walked up Tillets Lane, out the top and down to Pound Corner. Here he would have turned left and travelled past the entrance to the Beasleys on the left, on to Northlands crossroads; then he would have turned left at the junction on to the London-Bognor road. Following this to Clemsfold roundabout, he would then have turned left at the Horsham sign, then reaching Strood lane, signposted Warnham. Here he would have entered the lane, passing the other lodge on the left, and continued to Old Denne corner, turning left to return to Byfleets lane, thence to the starting point.

This route enclosed the whole of the estate. It should be noted that a few farms, smallholdings and houses were not part of the estate, although falling within its bounds.

The two lodges, one at either end of the drives, along with cottages to the rear of the house and other cottages at Stoney Hurst and in Tillets, and the Home Farm all housed estate employees. The Gregsons owned other accommodation, in Friday Street and on the estate land at the bottom of Friday Street.

Two old houses on the estate, although no longer there today, deserve mention. The first, always referred to as the 'Tin Bungalow', stood at the far corner of the field on the left, at the top of Tillets Lane. The only access was by the footpath or cart track. In the late 1920s, the occupants were the Jane family (see photographs on page 30). Mr. Harry George Jane was the village postman for a few years and

Mr. & Mrs H. G. Jane

*Edna and
Doreen Jane*

later, caretaker of the Village Hall. Of their two daughters, Doreen and Edna, the latter is the only surviving member of the family. She now lives in Auckland, New Zealand. Another family to occupy the house were the Capons, whose family were long-serving employees on the estate.

During the 1930s and World War II, various short-term occupants lived in the Tin Bungalow. There were times when Mrs. Gregson permitted homeless and destitute families to stay there. On the Carfax, she once picked up a family who had been evicted, and housed them in the Tin Bungalow. It was never a good dwelling, but was better than many at that period. After the war, Mrs. Gregson was frequently asked to have it pulled down. With no lighting, heating, sanitation or water supply, it was considered unfit for habitation. However, it was well into the 'forties before she agreed that the house should come down. She made an arrangement with Horsham District Council that, simultaneously with the bungalow's demolition, she be granted permission to build a house in Byfleets Lane. (The house near Chalk Ridge Farm was the result.)

The second old house, of much greater interest, stood in the last field on the right, as one followed the footpath en route from Tillets Lane to the Beasleys.

Hill House, or Marden as it was sometimes called, was originally a small farm or smallholding. Many similar, timber framed buildings going back to the thirteenth century, or later, can still be seen in Warnham village today.

As a boy, I well remember playing in and around this building, and I also remember Hill House being taken down. All the main timbers, roof stones, bricks and other parts had to be numbered. All the windows were latticed, and an upstairs one contained a stained glass panel with an armorial subject. The story went that Queen Elizabeth I had once stayed in the house, on her way to review the Fleet at Portsmouth, and the stained glass panel may well have served as a plaque commemorating her visit. The house was considered of sufficient historical interest to be bought and shipped to America.

Two other village stories lend further interest. One held that the house was possibly another source of food storage for the main house; the other, that it had served in its early days as a lookout or hideaway. Certainly the house was built during troublesome times, and its siting in such a remote spot, with difficult access, all made it into a place of mystery.

Records of its existence are still preserved, and positive proof of its location could be obtained by finding the deep well that once served the house. As far back as the 1930s, I found that the edges supporting the stone covering of the well were already crumbling. Another means of locating the site would be to find one of the many fruit trees that were in the garden. There was a large pear tree in the field in front of Hill House.

The problems that had faced Charles Bulpin Gregson in 1908, with the changeover to the use of mechanical land machinery and resultant loss of jobs to staff, took a different turn when war was declared in 1914. The war lasted five years, and involved the enlistment of almost every able-bodied man and many single women to serve in the forces. Others were needed to work in factories producing war vehicles or munitions.

Once again, the horse was to prove invaluable. With all the factories engaged in manufacturing war products, the production of agricultural machinery was halted. Making life even harder on the land, hundreds of horses were requisitioned for war. A vital part in the war was played by these horses. The numbers killed and the terrible conditions they were compelled to endure - cart horses, the best Suffolks, Shires and, indeed, any horse capable of pulling heavy loads - are sadly recorded for an unbelieving posterity.

Thoroughbred horses, which had been in use for racing, hunting and carriage work, were also commandeered for war.

Post-1918, the changeover from horses to steam and the motor engine took place. Although horses and steam-run vehicles continued to be seen on the streets until well into the 1930s, it was rare to see either for, by then, the motorised vehicle had virtually replaced them. It was possible to see all these different forms of transport functioning at the same time, for during the transitional period, each had its own special use. The complete changeover was to be spread over about fifteen years.

Chapter 5

Henry George Gregson
Molly's Husband

Henry, always referred to as Harry, was educated at South Lodge, Harrow, and Trinity College, Cambridge. At school, he showed himself to be a sportsman of considerable ability. The family still own a cricket ball encircled by a silver band bearing the inscription 'South Lodge v Bengeo - July 7th 1906 H G Gregson 136 not out'. Harry was only twelve years old at the time. In 1910, he played for Harrow in the Eton v Harrow match at Lords.

Harry also made 114 runs playing for Free Forresters at Trowbridge, in 1913.

When war came in 1914, he was commissioned as a Lieutenant in the Royal Wiltshire Yeomanry. It was largely due to his efforts (although he was ably assisted by Captains Charles Lucas and St. John [John] Lambert) that the Warnham branch of the British Legion - the Old Comrades Club - was formed. To get the club started and the Old Comrades Hut built, people were invited to buy five-shilling shares (they were to be repaid later). The original hut was erected by Jack Stanford, and was opened in 1919.*

In 1917, Harry became engaged to Edith Molly Mackay, and they were married in St James's Church, Trowbridge on 19th March, 1918.

It was replaced in 1954. The Warnham club used to be affiliated to the National British Legion, and only members of this could join. This changed some years ago and today the club is a thriving village centre, with over 1,000 members, including women.

WEDDING AT TROWBRIDGE.

LIEUTENANT A. G. GREGSON AND MISS MACKAY.

Exceptional interest was manifested in a wedding at the parish church, Trowbridge, on Tuesday, the bridegroom being Lieutenant A. G. Gregson, Royal Wiltshire Yeomanry, son of Mr. and Mrs Charles Gregson, Ends Place, Warnham, Sussex, and Calcutta, and Miss Molly Mackay, younger daughter of Major and Mrs. G. E. Mackay, of Kington Langley, and granddaughter of the late Mr. Alexander Mackay, of The Grange, Trowbridge. The bride, who was given away by her father, wore a gown of draped cream georgette, with crystal trimming, tulle veil, and a wreath of orange blossom. Her ornaments were a diamond pendant, the gift of her grandmother, and a diamond regimental brooch, the gift of the bridegroom, her bouquet was also his gift. The pages, Master Maxwell Farrar and Master Ivor Mackay (cousins of the bride), were dressed in white crepe de chine jumper suits. The bridesmaids were Miss Jean Mackay (sister of the bride) and Miss Kitty Scott. Their costumes were of nattier blue crepe de chine, gold shoes and stockings, with black tulle hats tied with gold ribbon, and their bouquets were tulips. The best man was Captain Jack Baines, Welsh Regiment. The ceremony was performed by the Rev. P. L. Puxley, Vicar of Westonbirt, assisted by Archdeacon Bodington, Vicar of Calne, and the Rev. P. A. Nash, Vicar of the parish. The address was given by Archdeacon Bodington. The service was fully choral, Mr. C. T. Weigall, F.C.O., being at the organ, and playing voluntaries while the congregation were assembling. The hymns were "The King of Love my shepherd is," "Love divine, all loves excelling," and "O God, our help in ages past." The bridegroom's father and mother being in India, were unable to be present. The bride's going away dress was of brown charmeuse with sable furs. The honeymoon is being spent at the residence in Sussex of the bridegroom's parents.

Local (Somerset) newspaper coverage of the wedding on 19th March, 1918 of George Gregson and Molly Mackay. (see over for the list of presents)

LIST OF PRESENTS.

Fitted dressing case, Bridegroom
Sable Stole, Major and Mrs. Mackay
Cheque, Mrs. Alexander Mackay
Brigg's umbrella and regimental Treasury note case, Miss Jean Mackay
Real lace, Miss Mackay
Diamond brooch, Dr. and Mrs. Lewarne
Brigg's shooting stick, Mr. and Mrs. Campbell Farrar
Diamond and catseye bracelet, Mrs. Ramsay and Miss Kitty Scott
Gold links, Mr. and Mrs. E. P. Alexander
Diamond brooch and cheque, Miss Ruddle Browne
Gold watch bracelet, Mrs. Ledger Hill, Mr Arthur Hill, Major G. D. Hill
Purse, Miss Betty and Mr. Teddy Alexander
Needlework, Miss Penelope and Miss Elspeth King
Table centre, Miss Iona Mackay
Brass Candlesticks, Miss Jessie Mackay
Rose bowl (Wedgwood), Miss Madge Rose
Silver milk jug, Rev. and Mrs. H. L. Puxley
Silver teaspoons, Col. Sir George and Lady Helme
Needlework, Miss Alley
Folding travelling clock, Mrs. and Miss Dickson
Luncheon basket, Capt. and Mrs V. T. Taylor
Volumes, by Whyte-Melville, Mr. Maurice and Miss Margery Taylor
Cake dish, Mr. and Mrs. George Tucker
Butter knife, Mr. and Mrs. J. Mountjoy
Cheque, Mr. and Mrs. L. de S. Brock
Japenese bowl and stand, Mr. and Mrs. Arthur Allfrey
Hunting crop, Miss Gladys Eykyn
Silver rose bowl, staff and foreman of Messrs. Palmer and Mackay, Trowbridge
Butter dish, Mr. and Mrs. Brown
Jam dish, Mr. Cox
Silver pepper castors, Mr. and Mrs. W. H. Kinneir
Rose bowl, Mr. and Mrs. and Miss Phillips
Purse, Miss Mary Selman
Cut-glass bowl, Mrs. G. F. Thompson
Needlework, Miss Rose Jackson
Coffee set, Major and Mrs. Reeves
Cheque, Dr. and Mrs. Briscoe
Gold buttons, Capt. and the Hon. Mrs. Allfrey
Dessert d'oyleys, Mrs. E. V. Booth
Morning tea service, Mr. and Mrs. Palairet
Attaché case, Mr. and Mrs. Mortimore Rooke
Address book, Mr. and Mrs. Watson
Handkerchiefs, Mrs. Alfred Tucker
Silver tea caddy, Lieut.-Col. Sir Audrey and the Hon. Lady Neeld
Silver breakfast dish, Mr. and Mrs. Geoffrey Peto
Silk scarf, Miss M. Ford
Afternoon tea knives, Mrs. and Miss Hobbs
Morning tea service, Dr. and Mrs. Tom Broscoe
Bread board, Mr. and Mrs. George Smith
Travelling clock, Lieut.-Col. M.G. Neeld
Cheque, Mrs. Lea- Smith
Cheque, Miss Lea-Smith
Silver trinket box, Mr. and Mrs. E. H. Clutterbuck
Rose bowl, Mr. and Mrs. George Little
Handkerchiefs, Mrs. C. Clarke
Diamond Brooch, Mrs. Charles Awdry

Pendant (minature), Mrs. Rigg
Walking stick, Lieut. C. de S. Brock, R. N.
Gold buckle, Mr. and Mrs. Cator
Silver frames, Mr. and Mrs. Martin
Amethyst and diamond brooch, Mr. and Mrs. Charles Garnett
Book rack, Capt W. Yockney and family
Stylographic pen, Miss Margery Rooke
Box (antique), Mrs. Armstrong
Silver toast-rack, Mr. and Mrs John Mortimore
Silver cream jug, Mr. and Mrs. W. J. Mann
Silver and pearl knife rests, Mr. and Mrs. Blick and family
Silver candlesticks, Mr. and Mrs. C. N. Jackson
Vanity bag, Major H.H. Willis
Toast-rack, Mr. Michael Sealey
Silver spoons, Mr. and Mrs. Page Phillips
Silver inkpot, Capt. and Mrs. Lysley
Hunting crop, from Compton Manor
Picture, Miss Donner
Copper pot and fern, St. Michael's Home
Silver tea caddy, Misses Agnes and Gladys Gordon
Brooch, Miss J. Campbell
Pendant, Mr. and Mrs. Percy Sylvester
Afternoon tea cloth, Mrs. Gaulter
Silver trinket box, Mr. and Mrs. Shorland
Ivory-bound Prayer Book, Rev. and Mrs. A. G. Copeman
Doulton jar, Miss E. Willis
Wedgewood jar, Mr. and Mrs. Kemp
Blue bowl, Mr. James Rogers
Silver and glass butter dish, servants at the Grange.
Silver sugar tongs, Florence
Book, Mrs. Campbell Laverton
Links, Miss Joan Coventry
Needlework picture, Miss Alison King
Water-colour picture, Mr. Ivar Mackay
China fox, Mr. Alick King
Leather Purse, Mr. Herbert and Miss Paul Lewarne
Gold curb bracelet, Mr. J. I. Storrar
Ruskin bowl, Mr. and Mrs. G. Wiltshire
Silver cake knife, Mr. and Mrs. F. King
Coffee set, Mr. Reay Mackay
Cheque, Mr and Mrs. Bagley
Work bag, Mrs. Page
Foot stool, Major and Mrs. Oakley
Silver candlestick, Mr. J. F. G. Froes
Hunting crop, Mr. Tom Newman
Clock, Capt. and Lady Margaret Spicer
Foot stool, Capt. and Mrs. Leatham
Silver salt cellars, Archdeacon and Mrs. Bodington
Silver and gilt sweet dishes, General and Mrs. Palmer
Pin cushion, Mrs. Havelock
Silver toast-rack, Rev. N. and Mrs. Thwaites
Embroidered handkerchief, Miss C. Kilby
Ivory-backed hair brushes, the Bride
Ivory-backed clothes brush, Miss J. Mackay
Silver ink-stand, Mr. E. W. Payne
Coffee and liqueur cup, Mrs. Broadfoot-Havelock
Silver salver presented to the bridegroom by the Offices of the Royal Wilts Yeomanry

Their first home was a cottage in Billingshurst. On 12th April, 1918, Harry's father died. He left Ends Place to Annie, although Harry was to be responsible for the running of the estate. The remainder of his father's assets passed to Harry, who was also responsible for managing all the joint family interests in India.

On 6th April, 1919, Molly gave birth to a son, Charles Bulpin, and on 8th June, 1921, to a second son, Geoffrey George Alexander.

One day after Geoffrey's birth on 8th June, Annie sold and conveyed all her property to Harry, having decided to move to Winkfield Place, Ascot, with her daughter, Margaret (Peggy). This meant that now, in addition to his father's inheritance, he owned all the India investments (he had already established some of his own there), including extensive Indian property and estates, the merchant-banking and stockbroking businesses, the private-investment companies, and a thriving racehorse stable.

In England, Harry owned the Ends Place estate, with its farms and cottages, livestock, and brood mares. Later he was to purchase Strood (in 1927) and Great Wildwood (in 1938) farms and cottages.

The Summer of 1921 was very hot, and in October Molly decided to accompany her husband to India (for the Prince of Wales' visit), and she stayed there for three months. She never went to India again.

After the First World War, for a few weeks Harry had joined his father in business in India. From then on, like his father, he spent much of his life out there. However, he returned to Ends Place for the summer of every year, actively running the farm and estate, including the training of his racehorses, some brought back from India, going to Scotland for the grouse - and playing cricket.

His interest in cricket led to his laying a special pitch at Ends Place, which allowed many fine invitation matches to be played there, fielding estate employees and gentlemen against the village team.* These had previously been played on the village cricket field on the August Bank Holiday each year. This match was guaranteed to attract a large crowd of village supporters. (My brothers - Eric, Jack and Bob and I all played in these matches but in different years. Bob was the only one to play at Ends Place.)

Harry took an active part in village activities, and he would have no doubt been at the forefront of things, had time allowed. He did establish a rifle range at the Old Comrades Club, a much appreciated facility.

In his absence, Molly looked after the bloodstock. No-one could have been better qualified to do so. Born and bred in Beaufort hunting country, riding to hounds at ten, she became a fine horsewoman and breeder of horses and hounds. Also with Molly's continuing support, Harry raced

Molly on the grouse moor in Scotland

---

* *see the only surviving cricket match record in Appendix E* horses in England and they had many successes both on the flat in summer and steeplechasing in winter. The latter was left entirely for Molly to organise, as Harry was away in India.

For the shooting in Scotland, he took a grouse moor every summer, and entertained friends there, mainly from India. There was always a large house-party, and Molly would join them. Charles and Geoffrey would travel up too, enjoying the company of the children of their father's friends.

In addition to the Scottish shooting, Ends Place offered much shooting of pheasants, duck, rabbits, partridges, pigeons, and other game. The annual shoots on the estate were an event from which the village boys could earn a few shillings a day as beaters. The day would usually end with a duck shoot round the ponds on the drive - at that time fairly clear of rushes.

Harry loved his annual return to Ends Place, and it is amazing how many engagements he managed to fit in, in just a few months. He liked very much to walk the estate with his dogs and a gun, to see what he could bag. He was an excellent shot and a reminder of those days is his fine pair of Powell shotguns, still in the family's possession.

When Harry was at home, great parties were held at Ends Place. Many guests came, staying for weekends or longer, and others came from neighbouring houses. Almost from the time that Charles Bulpin had taken up residence in Warnham, the annual party season saw great activity in all the country houses.

Ends Place was certainly no exception. A surviving employee recalled that all the staff, inside and out, would be "extremely busy". In addition to live-in staff, other help would be drawn from the village to assist daily. All preparations had to be completed by a certain time, after

The hall at Ends Place

which the maids would be closeted in their quarters, locked in by the housekeeper, who retained the key. Some of the "young gentlemen" were very lively, boisterous and noisy....Little sleep was possible as the parties usually went on until 3 or 4 o'clock in the morning!

Because so much clearing up had to be done the next day, the maids were usually called to start their day an hour earlier than usual - between four and five am. For some seasons, a special cook would be brought from London, "never a popular introduction as she was in control of the maids, and sometimes stayed for six months!" The maids slept two to a room.

The staff at Ends Place in those days consisted of one butler, two footmen, one head housemaid, one cook, three upstairs maids (including my cousin Muriel), and two kitchen maids (including my cousin Rose).

In the stables, two grooms attended the carriage - and a marvellous pair of horses. The head groom, gardener, butlers, cooks and head housemaid all had their own rooms.

I can well remember the hardships of life in the early 1920's for dozens of Warnham families, whose income depended entirely on employment on the land or in the house of the estates.

However, life in those days was not all gloom. People were much happier, more contented within their family life, considerate of each other, and generous when possible. Families would walk out together, picnic, generally entertain one another, and go to church. Children could be seen playing happily in the streets, fields and woods.

Many of our young days were spent in the fields and woods at Ends Place. Providing we did nothing to annoy the gamekeeper (Mr. Lion and later, Mr.Trask), we had the freedom of the estate. Carving names on trees, trampling crops or frightening game were the things likely to bring the gamekeeper after us. But picking mushrooms or hazelnuts, collecting birds' eggs and picking wild flowers (these two latter are unlawful today) and blackberrying were all allowed, and were pleasures.

Our regular play area included Tillets Lane, extending back to the Beasleys or beyond to Westbrook and the London to Bognor road. From there, we could wander right down to Strood Lane to Old Denne and Byfleets.

On the left side of Tillets Lane (no houses on either side, then), there was a wood that extended from Friday Street almost to Knob Hill junction at the top. The wood was mostly of hazel, and we often saw woodcutters at work there, coppicing during the winter. (Climbing trees was a regular pursuit, with a few 'favourites' in Tillets Lane.)

As with many other areas on the estate, in spring this wood was carpeted with primroses, bluebells and anemones - generally seen at their best in regularly coppiced woods. Before World War II, due to the agricultural depression, many fields were not cultivated, and so many wild flowers flourished in the fields, too.

Elderly Jack Nightingale could be seen most winters, coppicing in one of the many spinneys around the lanes, as well as applying his skill as a hedge layer. He also used hazel to make bean poles, pea boughs, tool handles, clothes posts, and sheepfolds. The gypsies would collect offcuts from his work to make their pegs.

Because of its abundance of trees and hedges, the estate contained a wide variety of birds and other wildlife. Apart from those along the drive, there were few ponds of interest but enough for us village boys to try our skill at retrieving moorhen eggs, using a spoon tied to the end of a stick.

There were few otters to be found. I followed many hunts along the river to the rear of the house, but personally never saw one caught. The largest otter caught on the estate, at Westbrook, weighed twenty-four pounds. The best view I ever had of otters, and a rare one, was at Westbrook. I was quietly sitting by the River Wey, and saw a family of four, playing.

Walking the estate lanes and drives during the spring-flower season was a pleasure enjoyed by many families, but when summer came, a large number of footpaths were put to good use - very interesting to walk there if harvesting was in progress, when we could watch the men working the horses, binder and haywains. In the school holidays, families or just children would spend a day and picnic in the field.

Who could wish for a better setting? Undulating fields and woods showing a grand splendour of colour - the gold of corn, mingled with early tinges of autumn.

In preparation for the harvest, the men had been busy the previous day, scything round the edge of the field to a width of about ten feet. This made a way for the horses and binder to travel, unobstructed. The corn was picked up and placed against the hedge or fence to dry.

Weather permitting, the horse and binder would arrive and, depending on the size of the field to be cut, the task would be completed in one to three days. As the sheaves were ejected from the binder, farm workers would follow and stand them in stooks of eight, so arranged to drain off any rainfall before drying was complete.When dry, they would be carted to the haywain, drawn by a team of two, three or four horses - a marvellous sight, to be stored in a barn or in stacks similar to haystacks. All the stacks had to be thatched, another lovely sight to see, and one now only seen in books since most crops today are gathered by combine harvester.

The stored crop would then have to wait for the threshing machine, mechanically operated by the steam engine that had brought it. The whole process provided a worrying time for the farmer, but a *wonderful* time for the children. They chased rabbits escaping from the cornfield, then, with the thresher disturbing mice in the barn, scampered after them as they dropped through the slatted base.

After the annual summer Flower Show, coupled with a sports day, side-shows and a large funfair, there was the harvest. Then came the Harvest Festival in St. Margaret's Church.

There was so much to see and do in the country that the days never seemed long enough, and there was certainly no time to be bored. And the climax of the summer was the harvest time, clearly remembered from my young days, when Harry and Molly were in residence at Ends Place...

When World War II broke out, Harry organised the local unit of the Home Guard, based at the Old Comrades Hut.

Then, in 1944, tragedy struck. Harry learned that Charles, his elder son, had been killed in action at Ravenna, Italy. His death proved to be a great shock and, by 1946, he had become very much a recluse, with little enthusiasm for any of his earlier interests. He was never again to be in good health. Asthma had always been a problem - no doubt, one of the reasons why he spent the winters away from England. He had also become increasingly deaf.

The one interest he retained was in his racehorses. At the beginning of the war, he had bought a large number of horses and foals from Mr. W. H. Hutchinson, the publisher. Harry travelled with Mr. Foran, his groom, in a cattle truck to Marlborough to pick up a load of mares and foals, along with a large amount of saddlery.

Thus, after the war, when racing was resumed, he already had a large string of horses. His pre-war stables, where Cecil Young had trained for him at Alfriston, had gone but, with Colonel Jickling and John Bailey of Wisborough Green, he set up Alec Kerr as trainer at Coldharbour, on the North Downs.

Alec Kerr had been severely injured while riding one of Molly's horses at Wye - a fall caused by too many horses having insufficient room at the first hurdle. After being ridden over by many other horses, Alec was carried back to the weighing room. Jack O'Donoghue, who had also ridden in the race, thought that Alec was dead. He did recover, however, but could never ride again. One day, Harry said to him: "How would you like to come and train for me and Molly?" He agreed, and their partnership proved to be long and very successful.

The many trips to Coldharbour and to the races, with Alec driving, no doubt helped to alleviate Harry's sadness over Charles's death. Always smiling, Harry was very popular on the racecourse, and well known at most courses.

Even before the war, as we have seen, Harry and Molly had considerable interests and connections in racing, both in India and in England. Friends from India were not only invited to shoot grouse in Scotland but to stay for 'Glorious Goodwood' week. Harry had his own private marquee there. and would entertain with lunch parties every day. There was always a large house-party at Ends Place during Goodwood Week, still recognised as an excuse for a great social gathering. His hospitality was legendary, but parties became much less frequent after the death of Charles.

Harry died on 26th November, 1957. He had left instructions that, following a service at St. Margaret's, Warnham, he should be cremated, and his ashes, ploughed into the field nearest to the village (generally known as the pump field). These wishes were carried out by his head tractor driver, Mr. Bill Carver.

Only two days before Harry died, one of his horses, Moretons, who had won many races for him, won at Fontwell. (This home-bred horse was named after his Harrow House.)

Sadly, most of the best horses had to be sold to clear the death duties. This was a great blow to Molly and Geoffrey, as well as to Alec Kerr. However, they did manage to retain mares and foals, from which they started successfully racing again.

Harry's death was a great loss to all concerned, only compensated for by the survival of Molly for a further twenty-eight years.

Chapter 6

Molly

Molly was born at Kington Langley, near Chippenham, Wiltshire, on 1st October, 1897. Her parents were George Eric Mackay and Kate (Kitty) Mackay.

The Mackay family were descendants of Lt. General Hugh Mackay, who went to Ireland to serve under King William II of Orange ('King Billy'). Perhaps influenced by that background, Molly was to remain a staunch Protestant all her life.

Molly had a younger sister, Jean.*

In those days Trowbridge, where the family cloth mill was situated, was the centre of the wool trade in south-west England. The cloth mill in its earliest day had been controlled by John Edgewell, predecessor of Samuel Brown, who was an ancestor of Sir Roger Brown. At one stage, Isaac Pitman** was a clerk in the counting house until he was sixteen, and his father was overseer in the factory. The firm produced very high quality merchandise, specialising in

---

Jean, always known as Sally, married Col. William Horace Mann, the son of W. J. Mann, a Solicitor. Col. Mann was a prominent soldier in the Wiltshire Yeomanry. He joined up at nineteen and served in the First World War, being wounded in 1917 and invalided out of the army. Years of suffering followed, and he finally died in 1938, aged 59. Among the many honours he received for bravery were the Military Cross, Legion of Honour, Crown of Italy, and the Star and Crown of Belgium. They had two children, Roger and Rosemary.

**Isaac Pitman (1813-1897) : Educator and inventor of the shorthand system named for him. He worked in the mill prior to attending teachers' training college in 1831.*

(above) Molly washing Ginger in the sea at West Bay, 1916,
(below) Molly on Ballet Dancer, West Bay, 1915

Cavalry twill, billiard table cloth, and light tweed. They were congratulated on the high quality of their cloth by King George V and Queen Mary, when they visited the mill in 1917. During this visit, Molly and other members of the family were presented to their Majesties.

THE ROYAL VISIT TO WILTSHIRE

Court Circular.

BUCKINGHAM PALACE, Nov. 9.

This morning The King and Queen, with the members of Their Household in attendance, arrived by train at Bath, and were received by the Marquess of Bath (Lord Lieutenant of Somerset), who presented the Mayor and Mayoress, the Town Clerk, the High Sheriff, and Colonel L. C. Koe, Commanding No. 8 District, with his Staff.

His Majesty inspected a Guard of Honour from No. 18 Officer Cadet Battalion.

The King and Queen proceeded to the Works of Messrs. Stothert and Pitt, Ltd., and were received by the Chairman, the Deputy Chairman, the Directors, and Managing Directors.

Having inspected the Works, Their Majesties visited the Bath War Hospital, where the Commandant and his Staff had the honour of being presented.

The King and Queen then drove to the Grand Pump Room, where the Mayor presented the Chairman of the Baths Committee, the Directors of the Baths, the Mayor Designate, and other prominent War Workers.

On leaving Bath, Their Majesties proceeded by motor-car to Trowbridge Town Hall, and were there received by the Right Hon. Walter Long M.P., the Lady Doreen Long, and the Hon. Geoffrey Howard, M.P.

The Chairman of the Urban District Council and representatives of Firms and of Local Associations had the honour of being presented to The King and Queen.

Their Majesties were then conducted over Messrs. Palmer and Mackay's Cloth Factory by the Manager.

At the Works The King inspected a Guard of Honour from No. 1 R.G.A. Officers' Cadet School and from the 1st Wiltshire Volunteer Regiment.

*from **The Times**, 10th November, 1917*

Apart from the quality of their products, Palmer and Mackay were recognised as fine employers. It is on record that eight employees had served a total of 376 years, that is, an average of forty-seven years each. At the time of the royal visit, the mill's output was almost entirely of khaki for the forces.

The other partner in Palmer and Mackay, Captain Anthony (Tony) Palmer, of the Royal Wiltshire Yeomanry, A.D.C. to the Governor of Madras, was killed at Amiens in 1916. The partnership then devolved to Major General Llewellyn Palmer.

All the family, including Molly and Jean, had shares in the business. It continued as Palmer and Mackay until 1949, when it amalgamated with the West of England Cloth Company.

Geoffrey, who was regularly to stay with Grandfather George Mackay at Kington Langley (where he hunted on foot as a boy, with the Beaufort Hounds) remembers his grandfather as he appeared then "an old man, slightly lame from a hunting fall in the 1914/18 war, who walked with a stick". In fact, George Mackay was even then extremely fit. He hunted, fished and shot, and was "a very wise man".

Granny Kitty Mackay, born 13th January, 1873, died in March, 1930, and was buried under a Celtic Cross, close to the lynch gate to Kington Langley Church. Geoffrey remembers her as "a kindly person, large in stature, who loved her garden and rarely left it". Grandfather Mackay died in September, 1944, and was buried next to his wife.

Their house at Kington Langley was very Victorian! In the 1920's, it was without electricity and telephone, and every member of the household and guests had their own candle to take to bed, and a silver ring into which the napkin had to be carefully refolded and replaced after meals.

Making hay at Kington Langley

Kington Langley - the house

When the telephone finally came to 'The Firs',* it was a peculiar gadget: a box on the wall, with a handle to crank when it had to be used. It was also necessary to hold the mouthpiece in one hand and the receiver in the other, and "it all seemed a great joke", recalls Geoffrey, "trying to get the thing to work at all". The walls of the old house were covered in pictures, many by Ruskin and other well known artists. There appeared to be thousands of watercolours, and portraits of everyone (many of the pictures are now hung in Geoffrey's house). Within the house, there was also a fine library of Wiltshire history books.

It was in this house that Molly Mackay met Harry Gregson, serving in the Wiltshire Yeomanry - although George Mackay was then commanding the Chippenham Company of the Wiltshire Regiment.

At a very early age, Molly had learned to ride, and showed great interest in foxhunting. At twelve, she was already riding with the Duke of Beaufort's hounds when her father took a fall, which broke his leg, after which he was laid up for weeks, and subsequently, lame. In 1917, she was the sole witness to a kill at Sandridge: she had been riding a bicycle, which enabled her to negotiate the country better. (The true reason for her 'usefulness' on that occasion was perhaps that she was more familiar with the unfashionable area than were the huntsmen.)

In 1917, she herself had a nasty fall at Widdicombe Mill, dislocating a shoulder. A doctor jerked it back into place on the spot and she was soon in action again. That same year, she was appointed joint whipper-in with Lady Blanche Somerset. In those days, it was almost unheard of for females to be made whippers-in. Molly also set a trend by

---

* *The house was left to Molly, who loaned it to Geoffrey when he married Anne.*

riding astride her horse from her early days: most unusual then.*

From then on, for the next seventy years, Molly's life was to be connected with horses, hounds, hunting, racing and breeding, and farming.

The great love of horses which brought Harry and Molly together led to them having many successes racing in England and India. The first horse which Molly owned gave her her first racing success. Baoudo, winning at Wye in 1920 in a two-mile hurdle race, had D. Casey in the saddle. This horse had been brought back, among others, from India.

From those early years, their winners are too numerous to list, but they included Irish Field (which won the Punchestown Chase), Monnika, Border Ranger, Stronsay, Craggie Rook, Henty, Quenton Lass, Ugly Gosling, Sunny Wood, Spontoon, and Nairn.

Molly and Harry were racing on the flat, hurdling, steeplechasing, point-to-pointing, and pony racing. It was in the days when the well known jockeys such as Beasley, Smirke, Elliott, Perryman, O'Donoghue and Weston were riding, and the famous Gordon Richards was among jockeys who rode for them.

The many horses bred by Molly could be seen grazing along the drive at Ends Place. Some, of course, were work horses for the farms. In addition, before the car completely took over, horses were used singly or in pairs, for the carts and carriages. Many tears were shed when Charles Bulpin's

---

* *When Molly was in her 'teens, before her marriage, she loaned her favourite horse, Ballet Dancer, to Captain Frank Spicer of Spye Park, Chippenham. He took the horse to France with the Wiltshire Yeomanry, during the First World War. Ballet Dancer survived the war and was ridden again by Molly with the Duke of Beaufort's hounds, in 1917, when Molly whipped-in to Tom Newman, Huntsman to the Beaufort hounds, of which the 9th Duke was then Master.*

G. Duke on Border Ranger winning the Hyacinth Open Handicap Hurdle at Sandown in the early 1920s

finest pair were sent to the First World War in France, never to be heard of again.

Molly was an avid collector of statistics, whether from newspapers, magazines, or notes from the many clubs, societies and charities with which she was concerned. Her own diaries reflect this lifelong hobby and from them, it is easy to discover that by the age of fourteen, hunting had become her great interest.

It was in 1913-14, while she was at school in Eastbourne, that she began 'The History of the origin of the Duke of Beaufort's Hunt'. It appears that it was not until the Third Duke rode at Badminton that any definite history of the hounds could be found. He had succeeded his father in 1714 and within fourteen years, there was a kennel book. The bulk of his pack consisted of harriers and six couples of deer hounds. The Duke showed a preference for staghounds, and it was not long before he gave up the harriers.

In 1745, the Third Duke died. He was succeeded by his brother, who seems not to have upheld the sporting expectations of his family. However, the hounds were kept on until his death in 1756, when his son, Henry, was twelve years old. It was Henry who, after a bad day out with the stag, turned his hounds to foxhunting and in 1770, the Fifth Duke took over the Heythrop Country from Lord Foley.

The fox was a much fitter animal then. With far less game on which to feed, it meant he had to travel further for food, but this gave him two advantages over the hunt: one was that he had better knowledge of the country and the other, that it kept him in excellent condition.

The Sixth Duke of Beaufort succeeded his father in 1803, and kept the hounds on. He resigned as Master in 1835, a year before his death. Both the Fifth and Sixth Dukes had been keen breeders of hounds.

By the end of the eighteenth century, the Badminton kennel was one of the best in the country.

All this was set down by Molly in a school exercise book, at the age of fourteen.

It was in the 1930s, when the Tenth Duke of Beaufort considered the motor car to be interfering with the hunt, that he requested followers not to use them, as the exhaust fumes and noise were spoiling the scent.

In her early diaries, Molly praised the Duke's huntsmen, who succeeded in raising the standard of his hounds, writing that great packs of hounds will always be found to have great huntsmen.

She was to prove this herself in later years, as Master of the Crawley and Horsham Pack.

Molly had a great dislike of barbed wire. In her diaries, she named ten large estates and their owners who, to ensure safety when hunting, did not use it, and recorded that many lives of great horsemen and gallant horses had been killed by 'this poisonous stuff'.

In describing the qualities to be looked for in a hound, she stated that only after years of experience of breeding can high standards be achieved. (In later years, the knowledge Molly had gained through the study of horses and hounds was remarkable, and rewarded her with many honours.)

Molly concluded her 2,500 word personal history of the Dukes of Beaufort Hunt with a Roll of Honour of members of the Hunt who gave their lives in the 1914-1918 war. When she finished the history, she was only sixteen.

Having been brought up in Beaufort country and regularly ridden to hounds there, was certainly the reason why the Duke of Beaufort wrote to Lord Leconfield at Petworth Park in 1919, endorsing Molly's enthusiasm for horses and hounds, and in a very short time thereafter she was established as a member of the Crawley and Horsham Hunt.

In the season, she sometimes hunted five days a week and she became very knowledgeable as to where they could or could not go. Hunting the whole of West Sussex, she nevertheless retained her interest in West Country hunts.

Within a few years, she was breeding and developing her own pack of hounds, with puppies housed in her own kennels, to the rear of Ends Place. These bloodlines were eventually to win her many prizes, and became known throughout the country. It is difficult to know which gave her more pleasure - to breed champion hounds, or horses.

The 1920s and 1930s were the great hunting years at Ends Place. These included the otter hunts, with meets at the front of the house, by the Crowhurst Otter hounds.

Having attended many of these as a boy, I can remember what a lovely sight it was to see all the huntsmen in their bright red jackets, and the ladies in their black riding habits, some sitting side saddle, and the pack excitedly mixing with the dozens of villagers on the lawns, waiting for the order to move off. The usual stirrup cup was brought from the house by servants, together with tea and sandwiches. It was a question of stamina as to which of the foot followers could complete the day but, as boys, I know we were happy to pull a swede or mangold from the fields to make up for the long hours without proper food.

In the early 1930s, Lieutenant-Colonel R.W. McKergow and the Hon. C. Guy Cubitt were Joint Masters of the Crawley and Horsham Hunt. In 1933, Colonel McKergow retired and, on the outbreak of war, Guy Cubitt was called up.

Having assisted the Hunt Masters many times, Molly

Reg Hirons, First Whipper-in with hounds

reluctantly now became Master of the Crawley and Horsham Hunt and managed to keep the pack going during the war - a daunting task in times of rationing. At the time she took over, they were hunting most areas of West Sussex, including the South Downs. By the end of the war, she knew the owner of every field, most roadmen, and the names of every farmer's wife.

At one particular meet at Northlands Crossroads, the Crawley and Horsham hunted a fox for an hour in Denne Woods and eventually lost it in the woodlands. Finding another in the Beasley Wood, the hounds were quickly away through Hoopers Copse, across Mayes Park to Cox Farm, on through Durfold Glyll. Leaving Kingsfold on their left, they returned by the Beasley Wood, hunting well in the large woodland, pushing the fox away through Ends Place across Strood Park to Field Place, on through Broomwick to Warnham Court, the scent failing there, after a first-class hunt. I mention this day's hunt, one of many similar recorded, as the map shows that it almost completely encircled Warnham.

Also recorded was the fact that in 121 days' hunting, one season, the Crawley and Horsham killed 138 foxes. Incidentally, some foxes killed were found to be 'bobtailed', their brushes having been mostly cut off by the binder during harvest.

On many large estates, there was an 'evil doers' corner, where, displayed on a large board, would be the carcasses or skeletons of animals and birds considered harmful to the estate. This often showed a dozen species.

Escaped Coypu, originally from South America, were seen in Hampshire, Surrey and Sussex. One was resident in the lake in front of Ends Place, and was fairly tame. They were trapped for their fur, known as 'nutria'.

*Molly's black labrador, Muntham Quaint (No.3)
retrieving a pheasant to her owner in the Honorary
Members Stakes at the Utility Gun Dog Society's Cup
Finals, Hever Castle, Kent, May, 1938*

Continuing to hunt during the war, but in a much restricted form, Molly was happy to invite old friends and hunt members when on leave from the Forces, or any that were stationed near enough, to join her. She often said she kept the hunt going for them.

Some of Molly's other interests, responsibilities and achievements started from an early age. Chairing various committee meetings, showing and breeding Ayrshire cattle, with great success in the South of England agricultural shows, breeding retrievers and field trialling, she was at one time President of the Horsham Fat Stock Show. As such, it fell to her to present the prizes. As well as the Challenge Cup and special prizes, there were many other highly interesting events. These included: the Two-horse ploughing match, Tractor ploughing, Best foal, Two-wheel cart with single horse, Four-wheel cart with two horses, Best pair of horses,

Best single horse, Best groomed horse, Best kept every day double plough harness, Best tractor, Best hedging and ditching, Best milking over 18 years, Best mangolds, swedes, kale and turnips, Best dressed ploughman, Competitor with largest family, and Competitor serving the longest time on one farm. Sometimes, Molly presented the prizes to her own employees.

The Gregsons had long been buyers of 'best' cars and, from the early 1900s, had regularly purchased what today would certainly be prized as veteran vehicles. In the 1920s, the munitions factories once again reverted to producing cars, and Molly at the time bought her magnificent Hispano Suiza. Its approach was always recognised by the throaty roar of its engine. Molly was considered to be a fast driver but, as with most things she undertook, she was competent.

The Hispano Suiza was designed to carry six, but it frequently carried more. Molly recalled to me one occasion when, with trouble in Brighton during the General Strike, a request was made to Horsham police for help. Molly then packed ten policemen into her car and drove them down to reinforce the Brighton Police.

The Hispano Suiza

The 'Hispano' was Mr. Padwick's ('Paddy's') pride and joy. When it was required, he would deliver it to the front door. It was always quite spotless, involving him in considerable time and effort, in view of its regular use on the untarmac'ed drive and poor roads. The car had a blown exhaust fitted, which accounted for the noise...

Sadly, the car engine was donated to the war effort, installed in a boat used for the evacuation of Dunkirk, and never heard of again. The chassis was sold after the war for £10.

Molly continued to drive until her death. Her later vehicles, such as the Austin Gypsy and the Land Rover, were much slower. In the Land Rover, she was often to be seen parked, sitting and chatting to people in the village.

Even in her ninetieth year she still had her great love for horses and hounds, and was still breeding award winners and attending many shows.

One of her last wishes was not to be fulfilled. Some twenty years before her death, prompted by her lifelong interest in her employees, the elderly and village residents in general, she had given a plot of land in Tillets Lane to the Council, to enable them to build houses and flats there, mainly for the elderly. It was her wish that she should make a similar gift, for the sum of £2,000 to £3,000, again stipulating that Council houses should be built, with tenancy preference for the older people of the village, and retiring Ends Place employees.

Discussions had been taking place for a year or two with this in mind, but because the land at that time was not scheduled for development, it was not until late in 1986 that completion seemed to be near. Unfortunately, Molly died before it was all settled and she could sign the agreement.

Chapter 7

Charles Bulpin Gregson
Molly's first son

The birth of a son to Mrs. H. G. Gregson on 6th April, 1919, at Ends Place was announced in *The Times* on 10th April, with a request to Indian papers to copy the announcement.

Charles Bulpin Gregson was named after his paternal grandfather,who had died the year before his birth.

As soon as he was old enough, Charles was sent to Lockers Park (Preparatory) School, Hemel Hempstead. From there, he went on to Harrow, into Moretons House, following in his father's footsteps.

At Lockers Park, he revealed great scholastic ability, and in most subjects showed much promise. He was always striving to achieve better marks than his peers. Few of them liked Latin, but Charles thoroughly enjoyed the subject, looking upon it as a great challenge to his intellect. He even tried out some Latin phrases when he wrote home to his mother.

Always needing to be in the forefront of activities, games offered him a chance to apply his energy and, to some extent, satisfy an early craving for excitement. Cricket greatly appealed to him, and letters home frequently reported success with 'bat and ball', not only in cricket but in racquets. He was also a proficient high-jumper, and a fine 120-yards hurdler.

Cricket, as we have seen, was a sport much enjoyed at home, and during the holidays he and Geoffrey keenly followed their father's cricket matches, joining in when allowed to.

Sometimes, their mother - an excellent shot - would accompany them, with her dogs, when the boys wandered round the estate with their - 410 shoguns, to see what they could bag, with Trask, the gamekeeper. Charles also loved to ride to hounds with his mother.

A special treat was being allowed to attend one of the estate shoots, to which many of their father's friends were invited.

If the boys were permitted to shoot, they were always put on the outside ring of guns, for safety.

Those were marvellous days, on holiday from Harrow, but they were numbered. With war approaching, both Charles and Geoffrey joined the Officers Training Corps and, according to Geoffrey, they all "marched about in uniform, and generally tried to behave themselves better than they normally did".

By this time, Charles was a house monitor, thoroughly respected and looked-up to, and was playing cricket for the house Second Eleven.

In 1938, he left Harrow, and again like his father, went to Cambridge, to Trinity Hall, to read law, where he "started his own little 'middle' career". He continued to be a fine scholar, and also to show promise in sport, as a cricketer, runner, soccer player and tennis player, and played football for his college.

He joined the University Air Squadron and did sufficient hours to qualify to go solo.

Chapter 8

Geoffrey George Alexander Gregson
Molly's Second Son

In its edition of 12th June, 1921, *The Times* announced that a second son had been born to Molly, the wife of H. G. Gregson, of Ends Place Warnham, on 8th June.

He was christened Geoffrey George Alexander - George after his paternal grandfather, and Alexander after his great great maternal grandfather. The ceremony, on 16th June, was conducted by the Revd. H. J. Tanner at Warnham Church.

Charles and Geoffrey on the sands at Seaford,
Sussex, in August, 1925

Geoffrey and Charles were always very close as brothers. Geoffrey went first to Lockers Park, then on to Harrow, in each case, following on two years after Charles.

When Geoffrey was only four months old, his parents went to India for the Princes of Wales' visit. His mother returned after a few months, never to go out there again. She detested the place.

As a young boy, Geoffrey recalls being surrounded by ladies - "some helpful, some not". During his infancy and pre-school days, a nanny and probably one or two nursemaids would have had the brothers in their care. In addition, there were a number of housemaids, kitchen staff, a cook, housekeeper and ladies' maid, all to be seen around the house. Should any have appeared to be 'unhelpful', it was because none would dare to encroach on the duties of nanny or nursemaid, who had to be strict disciplinarians to carry out parental instructions.

One of Geoffrey's earliest memories of Ends Place was the smell of wood smoke in a half-dark house. Wood was no doubt the main fuel for the many large, open fires which provided heat for the house. The high-ceilinged rooms of Ends Place necessitated the lighting of large fires, especially in winter.

Electricity was generated on site, but for lighting only. Geoffrey believes that the voltage so produced could not have been more than 112v, making the house always seem in semi darkness. The motor used to generate the power was a Lister, as was the machine for pumping the water supply for the house. The persistent chug, chug, chug of the two motors could be heard every morning and evening. Both were maintained by 'Paddy'.

The little boys saw little of their parents - who handed over their upbringing to pleasant, happy people, none of whom were relatives - not at all as children are brought up today.

As a child, Geoffrey could hardly remember what his

Charles, aged nine, and Geoffrey, aged seven

mother looked like. He dimly remembers her coming into his room to kiss him goodnight. She would also go into Charles's room at about six or seven in the evenings, and he would hear the murmur of their voices. Charles was older, and she obviously felt better able to confide in him. As the boys grew older, they were permitted downstairs into the drawing room to say good night.

He has many childhood memories of sounds that wafted up the stairs to their own little world in a corner of the house. For instance, he can remember the parties that were held. The ladies would leave the dining room when the port was served, retiring to the hall or drawing room. The gentlemen would move on to the billiard room, where they would play 'Slosh', a kind of billiard 'fives'. They also played snooker, or the quieter game of ordinary billiards, and these games often continued until three or four in the morning. These parties were the sequel to those held by their Grandfather CB, around 1910 to 1914.

During the school holidays, the boys spent a great deal of time out shooting. Geoffrey remembers shooting his first rabbit at a distance of only ten yards, when he was about six.

An interesting point is that the numbers of rabbits in those pre-war days were so great that farmers were pleased to have them shot or snared. The ferret was in constant use. It would not be unusual to walk quietly into a field in late afternoon or evening, and see twenty or more rabbits feeding or playing. Crops of corn, root vegetables and brassicas could be devastated by them, and their burrowing often spoiled banks, hedges and ditches.

On some days out shooting with a dog and polecat ferret, plus three guns, as many as sixty rabbits were killed. Geoffrey and Charles favoured the Rainbow Meadow and Strood Lane for this pastime, and would have had no problem finding targets there.

If they were not out roaming the estate, during the mornings they would be out on their ponies or would go hunting with their mother. As they grew older, the boys would sometimes ride to Warnham Station. There, having put their ponies on the train, they would travel with them to West Grinstead and hope to join the hunt, which often met at Knepp Castle, the home of the Burrell family. This was great hunting country, taking in the best part of the Weald.

In the Easter holidays, spring hunting on the Downs was the greatest fun. At the end of the day, they would "gallop back like mad" to Steyning or Bramber, to catch the train back to Warnham or Horsham Station, then ride back to Ends Place.

Evening rides by pony or on horseback from Warnham or Horsham Station presented no problems in those days, but would certainly be much more hazardous to attempt nowadays.

Remembering how cold and dark the house was, with its many passages, corners and rooms, Geoffrey records that during an exploratory wander along an upstairs passage, he was frozen with fear by the shadows thrown up, including those of the many stuffed, wild animals on the walls, which would probably have been trophies brought home from India.

Memories of his father are vague. He hardly ever saw him until he went to prep. school.

Once, during early childhood, Geoffrey was taken ill. Dr. Dew, a well known Horsham doctor, was called and Geoffrey remembers him whispering to his mother that he was "very sick indeed" - although he did not know what this meant. In fact, he had a ruptured appendix, from which few in those days ever survived. Two years later, his mother took him to Vevey in Switzerland. He still had an open stomach wound held together by clamps, and was also suffering from asthma. This was the only time she ever went abroad, apart from India.

Well remembered are the various governesses who tried to teach the boys French. Their efforts were quite unsuccessful, for their pupils just did not wish to learn. Geoffrey thinks that he and Charles must have been unpleasant to most of the governesses, as none seemed to stay for long.

On Sundays, at Lockers Park, they would walk along the banks of the Rive Gade and the Grand Union Canal which flowed through Hemel Hempstead. Wednesday was a 'half day', and was often spent "bug-hunting". Geoffrey amassed a lovely collection of caterpillars, moths and butterflies.

Geoffrey, pictured as Captain of the Lockers Park Soccer Team

At school, he enjoyed sport, especially cricket and football. He was captain of the soccer team and played in goal, which he felt was "an extraordinary position for a captain". During his two years as captain, he cannot remember his side being beaten.

At cricket, he bowled badly and was not much better with the bat. Perhaps he judged his performance too harshly, comparing his playing with that of his father, who was a fine cricketer. However, he thoroughly enjoyed the matches, especially the one when the School Eleven played the Fathers. His father visited the school on that occasion and his mother was also there, with Gladys Eyken.

Then Geoffrey went to Harrow, where he did not find the work difficult, but "did not do much of it, anyway"!

By 1937, the war looked inevitable and there seemed little point in swotting. At this stage, he had grown into "a thoroughly difficult, unpleasant small boy". He was a rebel in every sense of the word. He could see no point in passing exams, as well as not being good enough to be in the school sides. He considers that he must have been a perfect nuisance, and still wonders what Charles, who was a Monitor, must have thought of his behaviour.

Having left Harrow under something of a cloud, he returned to Ends Place to find his father was still in India, and his mother, quite impervious to the current world situation.

Soon after his return, he went to a 'crammer' for a few months, to prepare for Cambridge. He then went on to Seale Hayne Agricultural College in Devon, spending two or three terms there and learning something about farming. His idea was to join the army as soon as possible, then return to take up farming.

In 1938, Harry bought Wildwood Farm, Alford. Geoffrey remembers going to look at it with his father,

Charles, and Molly Moore, a friend of Charles'.

During one visit, he told his father that he would like to return there one day to farm. His father replied that that was one of the reasons why he had bought it. "With you farming here and Charles at Ends Place, you will be close to each other, and both on the land."

Chapter 9

Ends Place and its way of life

The house was self-contained, and the family had no need to go out for anything.

Both Charles and Geoffrey, while subject to some discipline at home, were spoiled children and, in consequence, did display bursts of bad temper.

Once, while Geoffrey was being prepared for confirmation, the Revd. Wholly, V.C., the Chaplain at Harrow, said to him: "Your brother nearly killed you once, didn't he?" Geoffrey countered with: "I beg your pardon!" Evidently Charles had confessed that during a fit of anger, he had knocked Geoffrey unconscious, and out of the punt into the lake.

On another occasion, Geoffrey had a terrible row with his housemaster, A. P. Boissier, who wrote a withering letter to his parents. Fortunately, Molly saw it first and threw it immediately on the fire, before Harry could read it.

When at home, the two boys had only a few lessons. They went hunting, shooting and riding - seldom, if ever, supervised. In the course of these activities, their courage was tested to the limit, and this was later to stand them in good stead. At the time, they knew no other way of life, and Geoffrey remembers being shocked when he went out into "the big, wide world".

Both sons were allowed £300 a year when they reached fourteen. Comparing this with a servant's pay of about £12 to £15 a year, with that of an estate labourer - £40, it can be seen how well off the boys were, from an early age. Indeed,

Ends Place in 1933

*Geoffrey at Eton, with Gladys Eyken,
his mother's lifelong friend*

money was never a problem to them. Many of their friends, too, at school and at home, enjoyed generous allowances from their parents.

Their father took them both to see the manager of the Westminster Bank (still in the Carfax) in Horsham. His name was Mr. Gregory. They were told "Woe betide you if you ever get overdrawn!"

This early lesson in finance was also to serve them well in the years that followed.

Even so, on occasion Charles and Geoffrey would borrow money from each other. Both had 'old banger' cars, which they loved to run around in, and it was sometimes necessary to ask each other for two shillings and elevenpence: the price of a gallon of petrol. In those days, petrol could be bought in the village, from a small garage opposite Warnham Stores and Cobblers Cottage. Rich Linfield, the garage proprietor, was a fine mechanic and engineer. The petrol was dispensed by cranking a handle on the pump. (see photographs, page 76)

As boys, they were always addressed as "Master Charles" and "Master Geoffrey". (Only after the war, when Geoffrey returned to Ends Place and was still addressed in the same manner, did it occur to him that he was "now not 'a somebody', but somebody else"...) When they were young and played cricket with the sons of estate workers or boys from the village, being addressed as "Master" seemed quite natural and they attached no importance to it. It was just as natural for them to call the others, men as well as boys, by their surnames and, in some cases, just by nickname.

In the house, there always seemed to be plenty of enjoyment, with people cheerfully cleaning the stairs, polishing the parquet floors and doing all the other endless household jobs. Charles and Geoffrey joined in the jollity, playing frequent practical jokes on the staff.

left;

Richard Linfield, sparring with his father, with brother Fred far right

below;

Warnham Stores and Cobblers Cottage (opposite Richard Linfield's garage and petrol pumps in the village)

Gladys Eyken, Molly's friend, made up the employees' weekly wages, and Molly paid them out. At Christmas, all the Christmas boxes were lined up on the billiards table in the house, with a plum pudding in a white china basin and a brace of rabbits for each, cash bonuses and other gifts. The staff would come in, touch their caps or curtsey, accept their presents and exchange Christmas greetings.

No expense was spared in the house. Geoffrey remembers great dinner parties, with fifteen to eighteen guests and the drinks flowing. Harry's hospitality was legendary. Molly was a lifetime teetotaller and non-smoker.

When their parents went racing, the boys were nearly always taken along. Molly usually had a runner at the various courses, and they wore Members' badges. Molly always took a brace of rabbits in the car boot, to give to the gateman at the car park entrance.

One day, the boys were driven into Horsham on a shopping trip by 'Paddy' (Mr. Padwick), the chauffeur. Geoffrey hated shopping but took a great interest in what was going on. As they passed through the Bishopric, he saw a long queue and asked Paddy what all the people were doing. Paddy replied: "Oh, they're drawing the dole". Geoffrey asked what this was and Paddy explained, saying that the people were unable to find work. To Geoffrey that seemed a shocking and extraordinary state of affairs. Here they were, always well provided for, while these people were queueing on the pavement, for work, or to get just enough money to buy food. It all seemed quite wrong...

Chapter 10

Molly - The War Years

In 1938, the Hon. Guy Cubitt, who by then had been Master of the Crawley and Horsham Foxhounds for two or three years, realised that, with war coming, as a Surrey and Sussex Yeoman he would be called on to take part. Molly was invited to take over from him as Master, and she decided to keep the hunt going. Those war years must have been very hard for her.

Charlie Denton, a professional huntsman, who had been hunting hounds for Guy Cubitt for two days out of four a week, agreed to continue under Molly. In her diaries, Molly describes him as 'a remarkable man, a terrific character'. Even during air raids, with planes overhead and bombs falling, he would always arrive at the meet on time.

Molly had accepted the job as Master with some reluctance. It was not because she did not think she could do it. She worried about how it would be paid for, or even if hunting would be possible during the war. However, it did continue to give much pleasure to any soldier who could spend a day or two hunting. It also offered relaxation to local farmers, and freedom for a while from their worries about growing more food, which for them was an ever increasing need.

Many of Molly's staff were called up for service in the Forces. She had practically no help in the kennels. Some assistance was available from older staff members. But Molly had to face the daily problems of exercising the horses and feeding the hounds herself, with limited help.

Charlie Denton

The introduction of petrol rationing presented the added problem of transport. Molly did have an old horsebox, a 1931 Vincent, made in Reading and inclined to be heavy on petrol. During the first year or two of the war, she was assisted with this by a Mr. Matthews of Brighton, who was a fine mechanic. Thanks to his care and maintenance, the horsebox never broke down.

With Molly driving, they frequently went off to meets, often three time a week, always arriving home safely at night. Unfortunately, when Matthews was called up, Molly was left with the extremely difficult task of attending to, *and* driving the Vincent all round Sussex. On one occasion, when she was travelling down Tower Hill, Horsham, a lorry with failing brakes overtook her at speed, causing causing her to swerve. The horse box flipped over on its side. Mercifully, neither she nor the horses were injured, but it must have been an alarming experience.

An additional duty accepted by Molly during the war was to serve on the War Agricultural Committee. Her job was to see that the farmers and landowners complied with the Ministry of Agriculture's instructions to plough the land and grow more and more wheat and potatoes. A percentage of each farmer's acreage had to be ploughed, and Molly had to check on this. The area on which she had to report stretched from Ends Place down to Cowfold, and consisted of many thousands of acres. It proved to be a great help that she knew by their Christian names the landowners, farmers and their children as well as most of the farm workers. The job was ideal for a woman in her position. However, after about three years, Molly found that she could not cope with all that it entailed, and she resigned.

Before the war, the house, grounds and farms at Ends Place had been well maintained. As the war continued, however, and more and more men were called up, pressures at home mounted and Molly had to give domestic matters all her attention.

Outside staff were soon reduced to the point where it

$\mathfrak{O}$n $\mathfrak{B}$ehalf of $\mathfrak{H}$is $\mathfrak{M}$ajesty's $\mathfrak{G}$overnment I wish to thank you for the service you have rendered to the nation during the war. $\mathfrak{T}$he task of $\mathfrak{B}$ritish agriculture, an arduous, indeed a vital one, was to keep the nation fed. $\mathfrak{W}$ith your help it has been done.

$\mathfrak{W}.\mathfrak{A}.\mathfrak{E}.\mathfrak{C}$'s by their care and consideration, secured the willing co-operation of the farming community, and have, by their energy and example, raised the production of our farms to a new high level.

I am confident you will always be proud of having played so important a part in the contribution which $\mathfrak{B}$ritish agriculture has made to our $\mathfrak{V}$ictory.

Q. J. Hudson

Minister of Agriculture and Fisheries,
8th May 1945.

To Mrs. H. G. Gregson.
MEMBER of the Horsham District Sub-Committee of the
West Sussex War Agricultural Executive Committee.

was no longer possible to tend the gardens, lawns, fruit trees and other trees, shrubs and flowerbeds to their usual high standard of elegance.

Mowing the lawn at Ends Place, 1941

The only help left in the kitchen garden was Gumbrill, who cycled daily from Horsham to Ends Place, regardless of the weather. Gumbrill's other duties included chopping kindling sticks and sawing logs for the numerous house fires. Before the war, he had been the 'garden boy'. He was still working at seventy, when the war ended, and he continued to do so until the 1950s.

The war years dragged on. Everything at Ends Place began to deteriorate; gardens, paths, hedges and ditches became overgrown, ponds filled up with weeds and rushes, and the drive developed numerous pot-holes. The lawns could not be cut. No petrol was allowed for mowing machines, and there was too much grass to consider cutting by hand mower. The kitchen garden was walled, and no machinery could be got in to till it, so the weeds took over...

Only a skeleton staff was available to farm the actual estate, and for them it was an extremely busy time. Throughout the country, the Women's Land Army were doing a great job. They were often not attached to any one employer and so could suddenly be called on to give assistance where it was most needed. They created much amusement among the old retainers. However, although lacking in experience, they proved willing and competent to do most of the tasks they were set. Without their contribution to Britain's war effort, the country's food problem would have been much worse.

The general public were of course playing their part, too, by digging up their lawns and flower beds, and growing vegetables. Many bred rabbits, chickens and ducks to supplement the meagre meat ration.

Chapter 11

Harry
and an Introduction to the War Years
1939-1945

For a year or so prior to the declaration of World War II, almost everyone in Britain was resigned to the fact (following Neville Chamberlain's peace mission to Hitler in 1938, and in spite of the famous speech he made on his return, about "peace in our time") that war was inevitable.

That year allowed a breathing space, for people to get ready for war. Everyone was advised to stock food, grow more garden produce, prepare blackout curtains and blinds for doors and windows, build shelters, and train in civil defence, with the Local Defence Volunteers or as fire watchers. Gas masks and rationing were introduced, women and children were evacuated from dangerous areas, and there was an urgent and important request for volunteers to join the Services.

All these and many other preparations took place, but of course this period also gave Germany time to strengthen further their already mighty war machine. Then, contrary to their promise, they marched into Poland, leaving Prime Minister Chamberlain no option but to declare war. This he did, in a speech to the nation at 11 am on 3rd September, 1939 on the 'wireless'. The race to get ready was then accelerated.

During the summer of 1939, Harry was spending his usual holiday at Ends Place, and he was at home when war was declared. After the outbreak of war, he formed the local Home Guard (who had taken over from the L.D.V.). Their first meeting place was a hut at the top of Tillets Lane. (Opposite was a mystery grave, and there were three stories told as to how it came to be there. One held that it was the grave of a gypsy; another, that a deserter from a previous army had been caught, shot and buried there; and the third, that a murderer had been caught and hung from the limb of an oak tree that overhung the spot.)

Warnham's Home Guard was one of hundreds of similar units being formed throughout the country. None were more active than those in the southern counties, where invasion by the Germans - particularly by parachute - appeared to be imminent. Indeed, one of the Home Guard's most important duties was to watch the sky for parachutists.

Looking back on those years, it seems unlikely that the thousands of volunteers would have survived, had there been an invasion. Few had any real weapons of defence, except for the odd old pistol and rifle. Most were armed only with shotguns, knives, garden forks, pitchforks, and tools. The fact that the Home Guard existed at all was because most of the men were past the age when they could volunteer for active service. But the spirit of the nation in those days was such that, with the exception of a few 'conscientious objectors', every citizen was anxious to become involved.

No doubt Harry and his men whiled away many hours chatting, enjoying a smoke and a drink, while keeping a watchful eye on the sky.

Chapter 12

Charles and Geoffrey Go To War

Charles's promising start at Cambridge was cut short in 1939, with the outbreak of war. He joined the Derbyshire Yeomanry, being absolved, as a Cambridge undergraduate, from taking the usual route via the Officers' Training Corps at Sandhurst. After a while, however, feeling dissatisfied with the situation, and wanting action, he transferred to the Commandos. Following a short training period, he was sent on secret sabotage work in the North Sea. He was in action in France at the time of Dunkirk, and was eventually evacuated from a place on the French coast, a little further north.

When he arrived back in England, Charles was sent to the South Downs, to join the Lancers. They lived in hurriedly found billets. Having been forced to return without their armoured vehicles, they continued to train around Findon and Muntham, in West Sussex. This was quite near home, and during that time Charles introduced many of his brother officers to his mother. When they had free time, they would all go hunting together, while waiting for the invasion.

Just before the war, Geoffrey went to Germany to improve his German. He was curious to know what the 'Hitler Youth' was all about. He stayed at a finishing school run by a Mr. and Mrs. Hammelmann at Stärnberg am See, in Bavaria. Their hosts had had many English students and were pro-British. It was clear that they were extremely worried about what was going on, and they spent every evening in their bedroom listening to the BBC World Service.

They also talked about a new "camp" at nearby Ravensbrück. Little did they know then that it was the women's prison and torture camp...Geoffrey was unimpressed by the 'Hitler Youth', but often wondered what happened to the Hammelmanns.

The period between his leaving Harrow and war being declared was one of little interest. Geoffrey just drifted along, like so many young people who have little or no idea what they want to do, or where they are going.

The declaration of war was to change him completely. He now knew exactly what he wanted to do. Until then, he had had everything he had ever wanted, in material terms. He was about to embark on a different way of life that he could not previously have imagined to exist.

Geoffrey had signed up many times, first when he was sixteen - putting his age down as seventeen. He had wanted to join the Royal Air Force, but he failed the colour-blindness test. Looking back, he realised that it was because he was colour blind (unable to distinguish red from green) that he had so often lost when playing snooker at Ends Place, by potting balls of the wrong colour.

Geoffrey was sent to the Royal Tank Regiment, in May, 1940, and went to Farnborough. Military camps were springing up all over the country, but Farnborough was a well established one for the army, and eminently suitable for the intake of new recruits.

They were billeted in barracks behind a public house known as 'The Dirty Dick' (which, he says, was aptly named). They were ordered to jump out of their beds at six o'clock in the morning and stand to attention by their beds for an inspection by the Corporal, who was extremely rude and knocked the men about if their beds were improperly made or untidy. Geoffrey survived his time there, 'survived' being the operative word. Great was the cultural shock...

After six months in the ranks, he was selected to go to Sandhurst as an officer cadet. The real war had just started. He found conditions at Sandhurst an improvement on those at Farnborough. Discipline was the same, but by then he had "got used to being bullied and shouted at, and it was like water off a duck's back".

He was posted to the Inns of Court Regiment. The course there lasted about six months (it was supposed to be twelve). His ambition was to go into an armoured regiment. Most of the cavalry regiments were in tanks, and perhaps he would find some friends who liked horses.

Now commissioned, he was sent to Ogbourne St. George, where he joined the 15th/16th Lancers, who had just returned from the Middle East and India, having had to leave their horses behind. They went to Luton, where "the streets were packed with trucks and Valentine tanks, much to the detriment of the kerbstones". From there, they went to Babraham Park, Cambridge.

It was the summer of 1941, and there was still racing at Newmarket, although it had closed almost everywhere else. This gave an opportunity to ride, as stable staff were in short supply. Ronnie Wallace, of the 2nd Royal Gloucester Hussars. was billeted at Bunbury Farm (now the National Stud), where he had a pack of beagles. Not much work was done and, after a disastrous exercise, 'Bumper', the Corps Commander, decided that the 6th Armoured Division would need another year's training. This was too much for Geoffrey and Michael Moule, who asked for a transfer, and got one.

Meanwhile, Geoffrey's brother officer, Mike de Chair, had married Anne Cobb, who was staying at Graham House, in Newmarket with her uncle, Bertie King; and Geoffrey had introduced Ronnie Wallace to his mother, a meeting which led to a lifelong friendship.

Geoffrey's next move was to Liverpool, where he boarded the SS Orontes, to join a large convoy in the Atlantic - destination unknown, but popularly rumoured to be Singapore. The convoy moved at the speed of its slowest vessel and was a sitting target for the pack of submarines which hunted it daily. After six weeks, the Orontes docked at Capetown, where the South Africans gave them a wonderful reception, welcoming them into their homes like long lost relations. From here, after ten days, they sailed on north and the popular rumour of Singapore proved wrong, for the Japanese had by now captured it.

The next stop was the Suez Canal, where they docked at Port Tewfic and from there, they went to the barracks at Abbassia, near Cairo.

One evening, Jim Agate, whose father owned the sawmills at Horsham Station, and Geoffrey went to Shepherd's Hotel in Cairo where, by pure chance they met Sir Peter Farquhar, who had been wounded and was on sick leave from the 9th Lancers. He had been a close hunting friend of Geoffrey's mother, and he suggested that both men should join his regiment, which was short of subalterns because of heavy casualties. Needless to say, neither needed to be asked twice. And so, from being being reinforcement officers to the Royal Armoured Corps, they proudly put on the 9th Lancers side cap.

Charles had gone out to Egypt with the 12th Lancers two months before. A build-up of Allied forces was necessitated by the large numbers of Axis troops, German and Italian, occupying much of North Africa. Geoffrey found his brother firmly established, and he appeared already to know the desert like the back of his hand. He had no need to refer to maps but had only to see the sun's position to know where he was.

The 12th Lancers, now well equipped with armoured cars and scout cars, were camped well south of the main coastal area of Egypt and Libya. Their orders were to find out where the enemy was most of the time but "not get killed if they could possibly avoid it...", although (pointed out Geoffrey) "such an order was extremely difficult to execute!"

Many battles were fought across the whole of North Africa, in a long campaign which raged back and forth. Ports and towns like Benghazi, Tripoli, Tobruk, Sidi Barani, Tunis and Mersa Matruth were names familiar to all those who were following the course of the war. Great battles were fought in all these, and many other places and the towns were taken, lost, and re-taken. Heavy losses were sustained by both sides.

In the early part of 1941, Tobruk had become a vital port, and the link to many lines had to be kept open, to Malta, and to other Mediterranean areas. Tobruk did later succumb to to a targeted, mass onslaught of German tanks and dive bombers, which lasted only two days. The losses from the battle amounted to twenty-three thousand British and Dominion troops, and a large quantity and of arms and stores. This was one of the events that shocked the British people most during the war. Similar battles were fought many times, but not with such success to the Axis troops.

Geoffrey's first job at Abassia had been to go back to Port Trewfic to de-grease the Grant, Sherman and Stuart tanks, which had been landed from the United States. It was July, 1942, and the work was very dirty and hard in the heat. Training continued with these new tanks until early October, when Geoffrey, Jim Agate and Otto Thwaites were each given a troop in 'C' Squadron, commanded by Major George Meyrick.

Until this time Rommel had been enjoying considerable success as Commander of the German forces, but now the Allied forces, under the new command of General Montgomery, were assembling behind El Alamein, ready for a major assault. They had been training for two months, and a new, optimistic spirit was abroad, with increasing confidence in the new tanks.

At Alamein, Charles was on the left flank of what was called the Eighth Army. It was made up of a large number of British divisions, with troops from Australia, New Zealand, South Africa, India, and France, plus a Free French contingent.

It was 'backs to the wall' and, with further retreat impossible, the troops were in their starting positions at 7:30 pm on the night of 23rd October, 1942. There followed a two-hour barrage of five hundred 25-pounder guns. It was said that, as if a single hand controlled them, all those guns roared out, tearing the sky into crimson shreds. With guns bouncing in their pits, new shells were rammed into the breach before they had come to rest; the whole earth shook with the endless concussions. During that first onslaught, the 1st Armoured Division moved up, in support of Sappers, through the minefields.

At 2am on the 24th October, in the bitter cold, the Regiment was ordered to advance up 'Moon Track' (a brilliant moon was shining that night), with Otto's troops leading 'C' Squadron. At first light, in spite of the barrage and the moonlight, the Regiment was still stuck in the mouth of the minefield, unable to deploy, and Otto was seen to be probing the desert - on foot - for a clear passage through the mines. As daylight came, it grew clear that there was plenty of trouble ahead, with burning tanks and trucks everywhere, and the infantry hardly dug in. They spent the day almost stationary, but the Regiment did manage to deploy a few yards and use its fire power to engage the enemy's 88mm guns, directly ahead.

Towards midday the enemy tanks appeared and must have been surprised by the new Sherman and Grant tank guns, which now outraged them for the first time. 'A' Squadron Crusaders fared badly, with their old short-range tank guns, and the Grants (nicknamed 'Ronsons' by the Germans) had also suffered. Jim Agate lost his Sherman tank and spent the rest of the day running back and forth carrying tank ammunition to the Squadron, from the ten-ton canvas-topped ammunition wagon. It was a very brave action. They 'leaguered'* that night where they had stopped shooting, filled up with fuel and ammunition, and crawled under their tanks to sleep in the sand.

The stalemate continued for another five days, with casualties growing on both sides. On the night of 29th/30th October, the 9th Lancers were ordered to withdraw to rest. 'C' Squadron's tank numbers were much reduced. Geoffrey's troop was down to two tanks; his troop Sergeant, Worswick, a wonderful regular 9th Lancer, had been killed with his crew, and they had suffered other casualties.

The new subalterns had gone to war in white cricket shirts, sitting on top of their tanks. They came out wiser, and sadder, but proud of their men and of themselves. A bond had been forged which would not be broken.

On 1st November, the Regiment were ordered back into line. There was no need for any 'pep' talk; it was obvious that this was 'do or die'. The Regiment crossed the start line before daylight, and halted while the Sussex Regiment advanced through their tanks, rifles at the high

---

* *to* leaguer, *or* laager *is the Afrikaans expression for taking up a defensive position at night*

port, singing 'Sussex by the Sea'. When light came, many lay dead across the desert.

That first day of November was the real killing day. Gun roared and tanks exploded. A German Panzer Division came straight at the 9th Lancers and 10th Hussars. Geoffrey's tank turret-ring seized with a direct hit and he was unable to traverse the gun. His tank gunner had been taken ill, and had been put on the tank floor. The wireless operator was now in the gunner's seat - it didn't matter: the wireless had been put out of action. A duel was being fought over eight hundred yards, with three Panzers and, when twilight came, neither side could claim victory. Geoffrey's tank was down to three rounds of tank ammunition and the last hour of fighting had been with the machine gun. By nightfall, thirteen direct hits had been scored on his tank, and it did not fight again.

The Regiment moved back in at dawn on 2nd November. The skyline was filled with smoking vehicles and, as the Regiment advanced, it became clear that victory was theirs, and the race to cut off Rommel's army was on.

On 4th November on Ruweisat Ridge, the rain came, and the enemy slipped away. The Regiment halted at Timini, too tired to think or count the cost.

Being attached to the same division, it was perhaps not surprising that Charles and Geoffrey should meet. This happened many times, by chance. Driving up a track, one would meet the other coming from the opposite direction.

The next few weeks were spent duck shooting in the bay below Ruweisat. The salt lake there seemed to be home for hundreds of the birds.

To Geoffrey's great joy, the 12th Lancers who had been camped on the left flank came over the ridge to shoot, and play poker, and among them was Charles.

Such breaks in the fighting were few but provided a welcome, relaxed break from hostilities and from the general boredom of not fighting.

Christmas came, with plenty of football matches. Charles and Johnny Henderson were posted to General Montgomery's Tactical Army H.Q., Charles, as a G3 and Johnny, as A.D.C. to General Montgomery.

In January, 1943, Major George Meyrick and Geoffrey, travelling up the coast road to play poker with Major Jack Price's 'A' Squadron, were hit by a tank transporter, irreverently known as a 'Queen Mary'. The jeep travelled at speed across the desert, somersaulted, and came to rest on top of George. Geoffrey was thrown clear, breaking his wrist. Fortunately, the Australian High Commissioner was also travelling up the road, and he managed to lift the jeep off Major Meyrick, and took both men to the Field Dressing Station at Barce. George Meyrick was badly injured, his leg became infected, and it was more than a year before he was able to return from England to command 'C' Squadron again, in Italy.

Geoffrey was luckier: after a spell in the 16th Scottish General Hospital in Cairo, he returned to the 9th Lancers, and was sent on staff jobs, with a spell as Liaison Officer with the Army Commander. The latter job involved reporting daily to the caravan, to be given details of the forward line, and any information General Montgomery required from there. This was a daunting task, as he never seemed to come back with the right answer! The caravan and mess were strictly non-smoking, and very little alcohol was allowed. All General Montgomery's staff were under twenty-five years of age. John Poston, 11th Hussars, was his Senior A.D.C. He had been in Moretons House at Harrow with both Charles and Geoffrey. Johnny Henderson, 12th Lancers, was his

Second Aide de Camp, Charles was in another mess near by.

Geoffrey was delighted in the spring to rejoin the Regiment on the Mareth line, north of Tripoli, where he met his cousin, Mick O'Cock (Peggy Tylden Wright's second son), who was in the Irish Guards. From there, it was on to the Cap Bon to join the 1st Army and the Americans, and to accept the surrender of Rommel's African troops.

The Regiment moved into winter quarters in Algiers, after a victory parade in Tunis, at which Winston Churchill took the salute, riding in General Montgomery's staff car, driven by John Poston. Both Charles and Geoffrey were present on this occasion.

The Regiment were billeted on a farm growing oranges, in a beautiful green and fertile plain. Leave was overdue, and Geoffrey drove to Cairo, hoping to meet Charles, who was on a Staff Officer's course at Haifa. They did not meet, but Geoffrey did do the Regimental Christmas shopping while he was there.

Meanwhile, the 9th Lancers were busy keeping everybody happy with a pack of hounds, hunted by Lieutenant-Colonel "Stug" Perry, and whipped-in by Roger Mostyn and Geoffrey. The intended quarry was a jackal, but the actual quarry was more often Arab Pie dogs, who kept running into their farms. Boar shooting with the French farmers was another sport, and a dangerous one, too. Otto Thwaites and Geoffrey set off on what they thought would be just one day, and found it extended to three - not too popular with the Adjutant, Francis Pym.

John Reid organised a cross-country course to test out the new tanks, which included the re-styled Stuart tanks, minus their turrets and now called 'Honeys'. When the day dawned, all the Generals arrived to watch but as it had been raining for three days, the event turned into an amusing disaster, with many tanks bogged or turned over.

Following his long service with the Eighth Army Tactical H.Q., now much reduced, Charles served on the staff of the 10th Armoured Corps. He was now to be continually in action on the Italian Front, having first landed at Salerno with the Eighth Army.

The invasion of Sicily took place in the spring of 1944, most of the troops being drawn from the Eighth Army. This Army by now was much reduced, divisions having been sent back to England for the invasion of France. The 2nd Armoured Brigade, with the 12th Lancers, remained in the Algiers area and it was with much relief that they started to move into Italy, after the fall of Sicily. The Regiment was split: some landed in the bay of Naples; the remainder, including Geoffrey, landed at Tarranto. This caused much confusion, and it was not until late spring that those on the west coast joined up with those on the east.

The next move was up the coast to the north of Ancona. Here, the Germans had dug in along the line of the river, to form what was known as the Gothic Line. By now, Geoffrey had been given the 'Recce Troop' with eight 'Honeys', and with Lieutenants Laurie Newman and Guy Hannen, succeeding each other, under his command. This was a wonderful job, although short-lived, and it was a great honour to be given it.

On 31st August, news came that the Gothic Line had been 'bounced' and the Regiment was ordered to move north as fast as possible, to reinforce. This message took some time to reach the 9th Lancers camped at Castellione, as Major Jack Price and Geoffrey discovered when they walked over to see Charles, at Tactical H.Q. Charles told them that the orders to move had gone out many hours before. The next four days were chaos. The 'Recce Troop' was ordered to lead the Regiment across mountain terrain and along appalling tracks. Tanks were consuming fuel at the rate of five gallons per mile and many ran out of fuel, or turned over.

It was 5th September - the 5th anniversary of Great Britain's declaration of war. The Regiment had re-formed and were in contact on the San Savino Ridge. The village looked quiet and deserted, and the 'Recce Troop' were ordered to advance to take a closer look. On reflection, Geoffrey remembered thinking that it looked too quiet! Creeping up the ridge, together with Corporal Smith's 'Honey', they had almost reached the village when all hell let loose. Cpl. Smith's tank was set on fire and it was with great difficulty that Geoffrey managed to pick up the crew. Meanwhile, the rest of the the troop had been engaged by intense fire and several 'Honeys' were hit, with casualties. Geoffrey's wireless was out of action, forcing him to make a serious error. He fired a Verey pistol to signal retreat, whereupon the world erupted, and it was obvious that they were surrounded by enemy infantry. The retreat was "hairy", to say the least, and it was not until many Germans had been killed that they got back. The 'Recce Troop' had been a fine football side, including Trooper Finney, of Preston, North End, and later, England, and Corporals Bayliff and Moffat, both 1st Division Club players, who were both killed. That was a bad day; one which Troop Sergeant Gates, a great leader and restorer of morale, said he would never forget.

The following day, Geoffrey went forward again to see if there were any more wounded to bring back, and bury the dead. Fighting continued for a further four or five days. When he went to reconnoitre again, he found the village full of dead, and the enemy, withdrawn over the ridge. It was here that he met Major Derek Allhuesen, 'B' Squadron Commander, also on foot (much to the annoyance of Col. "Stug" Perry, who was trying to reach him on his tank wireless). Next day, the Queen's Bays were ordered to advance, with disastrous results, being virtually destroyed by 88mm guns on the reverse side of the ridge.

Few of the fifty-three tanks returned. Geoffrey found the burned-out tank of Corporal Morris, with only the Muscovy duck 'found' by Morris and taken to the ridge with him, still there. (Bill Morris was later to work for both Geoffrey and Mrs. Undine Embiricos, in England.)

That was the last major tank battle the 9th Lancers fought in Italy.

Autumn turned to winter, and the Germans continued their retreat north, fighting a delaying action on every river line which Geoffrey's troop had to reconnoitre for tank crossings. It became more and more difficult as the rain fell and the waters rose. Finally, the Regiment lost its vehicles and were turned to infantry. "Going out on night patrol was no joy."

At Forli, Charles surprisingly turned up at the 9th Lancers mess one night in early November. He and Geoffrey had not met since the Gothic Line. He was on his way to command a squadron of the 27th Lancers, under Lt.-Col. Horsbrugh Porter, which he had just joined from Army H.Q. at Caserta, south of Naples. The brothers had a happy evening, and it was to be the last time that Geoffrey would see Charles alive.

On the evening of 28th November, 1944. the 9th Lancers were halted at the River Montone, unable to cross. Geoffrey went to bed that night disgusted with all the killing, and very depressed.

The following morning, his servant, "Smudger" Smith, brought him the news that Charles had been killed.

Early the previous day Charles, with the gallant action at Ravenna, had gone forward to help a 27th Lancers troop leader, who had been pinned down. Walking over to the officer's armoured car, he received virtually a direct hit from a mortar shell. He sustained severe injuries, and one side of his face had been blown away. He was taken back to the Regimental Aid Post, where he died on 1st December. It was from Col. Horsbrugh Porter at Regimental H.Q. that Geoffrey heard the full story of Charles's death.

Charles's grave in Cesena British
Empire Cemetary

They buried Charles in the Leaguer, with a simple white wooden cross at its head. He had seen five years of war, and had survived the long campaign in North Africa, with many hard-fought battles culminating in a victory for the Allies, and the defeat of Rommel's mighty army at El Alamein, which had brought him a bar for gallantry to add to his Military Cross. He had become street-wise and desert-wise. He had a brilliant brain and had experienced and seen what many men had not. He had taken numerous calculated risks, requiring great courage and, toward the end, he had written home to say that God, perhaps, was on his side. What a tragedy that such a man should be killed within a few months of the whole war ending. His brother officers told Geoffrey that Charles had had a premonition of death, "which I now feel he tried to convey to me on the wet night that he had dined in the 9th Lancers mess a fortnight before".

Life went on. In mid-December, 1944, with the Regiment held up by the continued mud and rain, making vehicle patrols impossible, Geoffrey went on leave to Rome. He spent Christmas there, comforted only by the Vatican Mass at St. Peter's, on Christmas Eve.

He returned to the Regiment to find that Major George Meyrick, his old Squadron leader, had recovered from his injuries and returned from England to take over the Squadron again from David Steel and that he, Geoffrey, was now Second Captain to him.

With the countryside drying out, the Regiment rolled north again. Orders were given to spare churches and historic buildings, as it became obvious that the fighting was coming to an end. The great German army was at least beaten, and surrendering. The Regiment crossed the Po in early May - and that was that.

The Italian countryside was in a poor state, with starving cattle and sheep to be see everywhere. The Italians themselves were in no better shape. Ironically, Geoffrey found a lovely chestnut mare which, when he was sent back to England, he gave to Jim Agate and George Rich, of the Queen's Bays. It later went on to win many races for them both.

Looking back, the Desert War had been a wonderful

experience. It was fought hard and clean, with no civilian population involved. The Eighth Army was there because they believed in what they were fighting for - freedom at home. The comradeship in the Regiment was something to treasure for life. Living close to men in a tank crew brought absolute trust in each other. When a friend was killed, tears were shed, and letters to wives and families at home were written. And the war went on.

The desert is a sterile place: there were no bugs to catch, apart from jaundice caused by sleeping in the cooling damp sand at night, and desert sores from the lack of vitamins. Illness was rare. The desert is also a lonely, but beautiful place.

Towards the end, the Regiment grew sick of all the killing, and when they met at Trieste with the Russian army, who had looted and raped their way through the Baltic States, they began to wonder what had been the purpose of it all. And should not the Russians now be defeated?

Geoffrey was granted compassionate leave and sailed from Naples to Liverpool in May, 1945. He travelled by train to London and stopped that night with Molly Moore, Charles' girlfriend (see Chapter 13), going on to Horsham the following day. He was met outside the front of Ends Place by his mother. She stood beside the place where the conservatory had been (it was destroyed by a bomb), Geoffrey was deeply shocked. Molly's hair had turned grey and her face was very lined. Almost her first words were "Things will never be the same". He found his father sitting quietly in his study, deeply moved.

Throughout their time away, both Charles and Geoffrey had written home regularly. Their letters, heavily censored and generally only possible by cable and wireless airgraph, or by standard Forces air lettergram service, on small postcards with small writing, transmitted as much information as possible and permissible. Their letters were eagerly awaited, and hundreds of them have been carefully preserved to this day by family and friends.

Now there would be no more letters.

With great pride, Geoffrey was summoned to Buckingham Palace in July, 1945, to receive Charles's Military Cross and Bar, and his own Military Cross, from King George VI.

Geoffrey was posted as Tactical Officer to Sandhurst, where he shared rooms in the old building with Hugh Rocksavage. On 29th November, 1945, he married Anne, Mike de Chair's widow, at St. George's Church, Hanover Square. He was then posted to Tactical School at Bovington, Dorset, under his old colleague, Col. "Stug" Perry. He resigned his commission in 1946.

Chapter 13

Charles - Man and Boy

The summary of Charles's life in previous pages does not adequately convey his personality.

To right this situation, I have taken extracts from some of the hundreds of letters he wrote while away from home - at school, college or wherever stationed in the army, even in the heart of military action. It all reflects a life, sadly cut short, that was full of energy and ambition, with some quieter undertones.

Charles himself admitted that he was of very restless disposition, always needing to be active. He considered this was entirely due to his sheltered upbringing, when little was denied him. He remarks imply that being completely spoiled was to blame for much of his early loneliness, boredom and inability to mix easily with others.

Much of his correspondence home refers to moods of depression. He was often angry with himself for his behaviour, then, full of apologies. Always aware of his failings, he was ever anxious to correct them.

There was however, another, completely different side to his character. As a lover of nature, he possessed the wonderful gift of appreciating all that he saw when out walking. On returning from holidays at home and later, following leave from the army, he would often take long walks to allay, or get rid of depression. After such walks, he had the ability to describe beautifully what he had seen.

One winter, while he was stationed in the north of

England, he walked with difficulty through snow that was very deep, marvelling at what he saw. At other times, in the spring and summer, when the countryside was coming alive, he would write of trees, shrubs and flowers in all their glory, in what really was poetic prose. Sometimes, he quoted poems which he had learned at school and considered relevant to his thoughts at the time.

From making a study of various of Charles's letters, during his brief days at Cambridge and while he was in the army, it is easy to see that an army career was ideally suited to his character. Obituary notices in the major newspapers, and letters from fellow officers and men under his command in the army, all praised his ability to lead and the quality of his leadership.

The only time when he was disenchanted with the army was during his early period of training, and when he had to move around to various parts of England, often living in most uncomfortable conditions.

Entering the army as one of the youngest officers, he suffered intense boredom at the outset. He frequently described those of higher rank as "old dodderers", spending far too much time in the club rooms, smoking and drinking, neither of which pastimes appealed to him. His life in the English camps was only made tolerable by short leaves or weekends away, which afforded him some relaxation.

He wrote that on a train journey north lasting three and a half hours, he had to listen to two ex-officers 'winning the war and settling everybody's future problems'. They had unpleasant voices but, worse than that, he objected to their ideas. At the end of that journey, he was surprised and annoyed to find that no one expected him at Long Eaton. Eventually, his posting was sorted out and he was settled into a camp where, he said, the Colonel was "the biggest bore in

England".

In Harrogate, when still with the Derbyshire Yeomanry, he wrote saying how much he hated the army and the war. This attitude was, in large part, due to the complete change in his living conditions and environment. Not only boredom but a swift realisation that he was quite unsuited where he was, led to his request for a transfer to the Commandos. He was also swayed by the fact that so many friends had already crossed the Channel to France, Belgium and Holland.

The news of his transfer was a great relief and must have dispelled his feelings of frustration. He was soon being sent on secret missions to Holland, where the war had reached a serious stage. His family and friends did not know exactly what he was doing.

Then came other postings, but it was not long before Charles was on board ship for Egypt. In letters, he recorded the cramped and overcrowded conditions, and he reflected on having left behind all those relations and friends, and the country he loved so much.

His letters always enquired after the family's health. How were they coping with rationing? How were his favourite horses and dogs? Was mother managing to keep the farm running smoothly? Was she still hunting, and able to keep the hounds fed?

The great love of his life was Molly Moore, of Maynes Park, Warnham. She shared his interest in hunting and shooting. He would sometimes ride her horses out hunting and probably enjoyed her company more than that of anybody else.

During his early army training, they would meet whenever leave allowed. Should they be some distance apart, they would meet halfway.

Charles was very concerned for Molly's safety, when her war work kept her frequently in London in the days of the blitz. Frequently expressing his love for her, he often spoke of marriage but it was not to be.

Charles's mother opposed the idea of their marriage, saying that he was too young. Aware of opposition at home, Charles wrote to Mollie from Yorkshire to say that on 6th April (1940) he would be twenty-one, and would like to marry her as soon as possible after that date.

About that time, both Charles and Mollie were sent abroad: Mollie, to France and Charles, to Egypt. They continued to correspond throughout the war years, right up until the time Charles was killed in action.

From the obituary column of *The Times*, dated 19th January. 1945:

Personal Tribute
Major C B Gregson

G.J.K. and R.H.P.* write:

The death of Major Charles Bulpin Gregson, M.C., in action in Italy, came as a great shock and caused very deep sorrow to his many friends. Educated at Harrow, he lived in the Crawley and Horsham country, where his mother still carries on as Master. His whole life was devoted to the country and what it stood for, and nothing pleased Charles more than a Sunday afternoon walk with his terriers and some friends. He came

---

* *Col. George Kitson and Major Rodney Palmer*

to the 12th Lancers in September 1941, from the Derbyshire Yeomanry, and at once made many friends. It was apparent from the first that he was an outstanding soldier. A magnificent leader, and utterly fearless, he earned his first M.C. at Knightsbridge, and a Bar at El Alamein when the advance was held up temporarily by some 80mm, and other guns. He worked round behind and went in at 200 yards, getting a beautiful right and left on an 80mm and 50mm. The remaining Germans had had enough and pulled out, and the advance of the division then continued. He then went on to the corps staff, where he was considered to be a brilliant young staff officer, and then on to the Staff College. After 18 months he returned once more to the battle, where he was killed on December 1 while commanding a squadron of the 27th Lancers, which he had just joined. His love of life and unfailing selflessness will ever remain in the memory of those who were lucky enough to serve with him. He had a great future as a soldier or in the peace and quiet of Sussex, where he lived.

Chapter 14

The Last Years at Ends Place

Now living at Kington Langley, Geoffrey went to the Royal Agricultural College at Cirencester, travelling daily from home. He found a Ministry of Agriculture post monitoring the acreage grants to farmers for growing potatoes, administered by the Ministry from Trowbridge. This involved visiting farms throughout Wiltshire, as well as studying at Cirencester. With the help of his demobilisation grant, and his unused army pay, he and Anne bought Haugh Farm, in Winsley, a village near Bradford on Avon.

At Haugh Farm, Geoffrey established a small grading-up herd of Ayrshire dairy cows, by purchasing in-calf heifers from Scotland, which in 1948 cost about £48 each. This was a very much a do-it-yourself enterprise, which Geoffrey and Anne ran on their own. It was a profitable and pleasant form af slavery and, much to the amazement of his friends and his father, they disappeared from the social scene in Wiltshire for about six years. By then, the dairy herd had outgrown the farm, and a sale and move became vital.

In 1954, they became tenants of Lord Cowdray at Lower Lodge Farm, near Fernhurst, in West Sussex. Here they set up an operation on a much larger scale, farming about 500 acres, milking around 100 cows, with an additional beef and arable enterprise. Geoffrey employed a full farm staff, enabling him to enjoy a lifestyle which, during the war years, he had only been able to dream of. He hunted with the Hampshire Hounds on Thursdays, mostly to qualify point-to-pointers, and ran a small shoot for his friends to enjoy.

Ends place was close at hand, so Geoffrey's mother, and father, when he was well enough, visited frequently. His mother especially liked the Ayrshire herd and gradually replaced the Ends Place Shorthorn herd with Geoffrey's Ayrshires.

Gladys Eyken was still a frequent visitor to Ends Place. Peggy Bannister was his father's secretary and kept the milk records at Strood farm. This was a new experience for them and caused much interest, because Molly rarely visited the dairy herd and certainly knew nothing of milk records just as, Geoffrey recalls, she scarcely knew where the kitchen at Ends Place was.

Life at Fernhurst was good, with the children - Charles, Mark and Nicola - growing up. The boys went to Harrow. Nicola was keen on ponies. Anne's parents and sisters lived nearby, at Stedham.

Mark, Nicola and Charles

The racing scene was growing more interesting, and Geoffrey had a marvellous 'chaser called Comforting Wave, which he had in training with Desmond McInnes-Skinner, an old friend from the 9th Lancers. Once the horse had finished his early career, Geoffrey had the 'chaser back. He was to win seventeen races before he had a fatal accident in a cross-country race, when Geoffrey was hunting the Tynedale Hounds, in Northumberland.

Sadly, those good times came to an end when Geoffrey and Anne decided to divorce. In 1958, he had bought Duchally, a hill sheep farm in Sutherland, at the source of the River Cassley. It was a lovely, wild place, under Ben More Assynt, twenty-four miles up the Glen on an unmetalled road, full of deer and otters which used to come to the river from Loch Shin.

One year, Charles and Mark went up to stay for Christmas, were snowed in, and missed the Easter term at Harrow. It took considerable persuasion to convince their Housemaster at Moretons that it was impossible to get south!

Many friends came to stay and stalk deer each year, among them Dr. Richard Hollick, whose widow now lives in Dorset, close to Geoffrey. Geoffrey had purchased Little Wildwood Farm, where he wintered his flock of black-faced lambs from Duchally.

Geoffrey later moved here with his horses from Lower Lodge, and was joined by Undine Embricos, whom he had known from his hunting days with the Hampshire and Chiddingfold and Leconfield hunts. A considerable 'goer' across country, she was following him in an evening hunt at Rotherfield Park when she had a heavy fall, fracturing her skull. She was unconscious for ten days in Lord Mayor Treloar's Hospital in Alton. On her recovery, she married Geoffrey.

The following season, that of 1965, Geoffrey was invited to become Master of the Hampshire Hounds, joining a syndicate of three others as Acting Masters for one season - which was stretched to ten! John Gray, a major yeoman farmer from Cheriton, Hampshire, was the lynchpin of this Mastership, which had various Joint Masters over the years. It was to him that Geoffrey finally handed the hounds over, in 1975, when he took the Tynedale in Northumberland.

These were extremely happy years for Geoffrey and Undine, whose two-year-old son had joined them at Little Wildwood Farm. They travelled in their horsebox from there to wherever hounds were meeting during the season, up to thirty-five miles, although later in the Mastership, the Hunt Club allowed him to use the Hunt Lodge when he was hunting hounds, and he could keep his horses at the kennels. John Gray was a tower of strength, and no bonafide farmer would refuse the hounds access, because of his popularity. (He also supplied Geoffrey with cigarettes at moments of stress!) Meanwhile Geoffrey, a keen shot himself, continued to look after the shooting interests in the hunting country.

By now, Molly had given up the Crawley and Horsham Hounds, and had been succeeded by David Sandeman. However, she became a keen foot follower, both of the Crawley and Horsham, and the Hampshire Hounds, and was often to be seen following the hunt in her Land-Rover.

Geoffrey and Undine loved the Tynedale. From 1974 to 1977, they rented a farmhouse close to the kennels and hunted hounds three days a week - and on other days as well - when it was barely fit to hunt! Eighteen horses were kept at Fenwick Shield and the kennels. Often, Geoffrey rode three horses during a days hunting. Undine crossed the country "at the speed of light" on anything that was sound. Her great horses, Token, Greyboy and Choice were still with her. There were plenty of foxes in the country, and they had to be caught because the farmers were concerned for the safety of their lambs. It was all 'white' grass and wonderful scenting, rarely requiring a 'cast' once the hounds were settled, and that magnificent pack of hounds were real fox-catchers. Tony Edwards was his kennel Huntsman, and was a very fine hunt servant. These were magical days indeed, sadly ending in 1977.

Molly had not entirely agreed with Geoffrey's to move to the Tynedale. It was at a time when her health was failing fast. For years, she had suffered from arthritis aggravated, no doubt, by hunting so often through the years in deplorable weather. Arthritis had been in the family for generations. Grandfather Mackay had it, and now Geoffrey is finding it an increasing handicap.

Eventually, it crippled Molly but with a wonderful old horse called Knuckleduster, she continued to go out. Knuckleduster had to be put down a few years after Molly gave up the Mastership, suffering from grass sickness. Molly, who had been so attached to the horse, never rode again.

Molly had found it increasingly difficult to get on to a horse during her last years hunting. Her arthritic affliction was not so much in her hips as in her knees, but it continued to spread over her body. Her hands became very bad, her fingers drawing right back. She soon found it impossible to carry on the active life she loved, and there came a time when she could really only get round in her Land-Rover.

A keen owner, breeder and follower of horse racing, in the year that Never Say Die won the Derby (1954) she said to Geoffrey "That's me!". She certainly lived for many years after that... She had many old retainers, faithful servants for many years, whom she kept on. Any who did leave usually

*Molly (holding four-year-old Primrose) in her Land-Rover,
with Reg Hirons and his terriers (1974)*

did so because they themselves felt past continuing. Those who stayed there would have found the house increasingly uncomfortable. Mr. Marshall, who used to manage the farm, lives in Warnham in Byfleets Lane to this day, as still do other former staff of Ends Place.

Girl grooms were in charge of the stable. Joyce and Grace were taking care of Molly in the house and living-in, as was her secretary, Marjorie, with her son William, until they found a cottage in the village. Capon had been a very capable man with heavy horses for many years, and was still able to cope, even at the age of eighty. He lived with his son, Jack, who also worked for a time for Geoffrey, in the Back Lodge. His mother was in good hands and Geoffrey had every confidence that she was being well looked after, when he was away in Northumberland.

Meanwhile, however, money problems had been growing: since the war, the farms had never produced sufficient money for their general maintenance and upkeep. Molly had to sell, at only a fair price, the herd of Ayrshire cattle, the milk from which had provided the main source of income.

Douglas Fox took over the running of the estate from King and Chasemore in 1958, and lived at Strood Wood. On checking the figures each year, it became obvious that Ends Place estate was getting further and further into financial trouble, and there seemed no easy solution.

It was suggested that Molly should return to her birth place, Kington Langley, and Geoffrey should go to Ends Place - a solution both of them rejected.

Meanwhile Geoffrey and Undine returned from Northumberland to Great Wildwood Farm. His son Charles and his wife, Caroline, previously living there, bought Heathers Farm at Bucks Green, where their sons, Oliver and

James, were born. Mr. and Mrs. Kelsey, who had managed Great Wildwood since 1938, moved to a modern house, in Alfold (almost opposite the farm driveway), built by Jack Standford.

Geoffrey converted Great Wildwood into one house, making it very comfortable, and considered that he could run the farms at both Ends Place and Great Wildwood. To this, his mother agreed - although Geoffrey knew it would not solve the financial problems. Under Harry's will, Molly could continue at Ends Place for her lifetime, with Geoffrey as "remainder man", which meant that he would inherit the estate on his mother's death. They were all aware that Molly was nearing the end of her life, and with the financial problems so pressing, she suggested to Geoffrey that if they had an offer on Ends Place, they should seriously consider it.

As it happened, Douglas Fox, who was also running the Lucas estate of Warnham Court, suggested that, as that estate had lost a lot of land when the Horsham by-pass was built and Charles Lucas was looking to expand his agricultural land holding before he died, they might well be interested in buying Ends Place. So it came about that Molly signed an agreement, of which Geoffrey approved, and the contract for the sale of Ends Place to the Lucas Trust was verbally agreed, just before she died.

Geoffrey and Undine settled in at Great Wildwood, following their return from Northumberland. They had made many improvements to the property and were getting the place into a profitable situation by doing much of the work themselves. They were also breeding from a number of mares, their foals giving them great pleasure.

In early November, 1988, as Molly sat watching the Cheltenham races on television, she collapsed back into her chair. Joyce helped to raise her but, as she did so, Molly slipped back with a massive stroke. Fortunately, Geoffrey was at home when he received the call, and he immediately went to Ends Place. Ben Longridge, the previous farm manager came to the house, and they managed to carry her up to her bedroom, although by then she was unconscious.

Geoffrey returned to Ends Place later that evening, but found that nothing could be done to help his mother, and she died early on the morning of Sunday, 10th November. He recalls standing in his mother's room, looking out of the window, hearing the Warnham Church bells ringing for Armistice Day, and thinking how very strange it was that everything happened to the Gregsons in November.

Only a month before, Molly had celebrated her ninetieth birthday with a large champagne party at Ends Place, for her many friends and family.

She was buried as she wished, in Warnham Churchyard. She had requested that no fuss should be made, and that the service should be private. Geoffrey, however, did not have the heart to stop people from attending the funeral. Indeed, he considered that he did not have the right to do so.

The service was a very sad occasion. Molly was much loved and respected throughout the village, and the church was full. The organist played "D'ye ken John Peel" as she was carried into the church.

Geoffrey and Undine returned to Ends Place with his son, Mark and Naomi, his wife, his daughter, Nicola, Geoffrey's cousins Roger and Rosemary Mann, and Mark Calvert-Lee, the Family Solicitor, and Ronnie Wallace. Geoffrey's eldest, Charles, was on business in the Far East.

The house seemed very empty when they all got back, with hardly a sound to be heard. There was a fire in the drawing room and Molly's favourite chair, in which she had spent countless hours with a cat or one or another of her terriers on her lap, now stood empty in front of the hearth. Many childhood memories flooded back, as Geoffrey stood there.

The outstanding bills were settled. Molly's straightforward Will left legacies to her grandchildren, and to many of her servants. The contract of the sale of Ends Place was completed and the Lucas Trust took over the estate. The house, gardens, front drive and lakes were subsequently re-sold by the Lucas Trust.

Geoffrey had expected the house to be restored and made into flats. It was indeed a sad day and a great disappointment, when he heard that it had been demolished, and a new house was subsequently being built on its site. From that day to this, he has not been back.

The Gregson era of over seventy years at Ends Place had come to an end.

APPENDICES

Appendix A

Molly's Hunting Journals

I have already mentioned Molly's introduction to hunting at a very early age, first in the West Country, then in Sussex. It was at Ends Place that hunting became the greatest interest in her life. Associated interests were the breeding of hunters and champion hounds. What she herself called 'the study of pedigree, performance and build of every animal' was of paramount importance to her.

It is no surprise, then, to find her Hunting Journals much greater in numbers than the Game Books at Ends Place. Although her personal diaries start earlier, her first Hunting Journal is dated 9th November, 1911. She realised that only Hunting Journals could provide her with an accurate record for her future hunting activities.

Riding with the Duke of Beaufort's hounds, she hunted twenty days during her first season, favouring two horses - Game Chicken and Robin Hood. By 1918, she had been out with the Duke's hounds one hundred and eighty times, as well as attending other hunts.

From the time that she joined the Crawley and Horsham hunt, her journals go into great detail as to horses ridden, their owners, their hounds, the places of meets, and the foxes that were found, lost or killed. She also mentions the kind of weather and type of country hunted.

Listed below are the names of the hunters she rode in the southern counties. The horses are listed in the chronological order in which they were ridden, with the number of rides of each, up until the start of World War II.

Name	T/R	Name	T/R
Monte Carlo	16	Rufus	2
Sandy	8	Sunny Wood	1
Josephine	6	Champagne	114
Brown Mare	5	Safety Raynor	6
Silence	3	Miss Long	11
The Flunkey	5	Nairn	56
Munster	2	Alarm	21
Sanford	1	Black Bess	1
Virginia	64	Rocket	1
Basil	8	Lorna	2
Ballet Dancer	43	Captive Balloon	54
Acid Drop	7	Unicorn	72
Tommy	2	Elegance	9
Bomb Shell	2	Herd	3
Ginger Beer	2	Ugly Gosling	46
Little Ginger	1	Quendon Lass	120
Brook	4	Yda	154
Call Boy	2	Blackie	125
Secret	18	Gold Flake	67
Jimmy	1	Hot Bun	1
Milk Sop	3	Standfast	6
Stella	4	Diamond Queen	23
Clonmel	1	Simonswood	5
Abu Ben Adem	40		1,155

T/R = Times Ridden

Many of the above were retired racehorses, winning numerous races, and were some of Molly's best breeding stock.

During all her riding years, Molly had few falls and only one serious one, which resulted in a broken pelvis.

Although she continued to hunt through the war years, it can be seen from her journals that less time was then available, but she continued to record briefly what she thought were vital comments. She mentions that the feeding of raw flesh to the hounds was quite satisfactory. Substitutes for any lack of food were supplied by mangolds, potatoes, crushed oats and maize gluten. She noted that the hounds looked well and kept their condition throughout the war.

A great number of meets were held at Knepp Castle, West Grinstead Park, the home of Sir Merrick Burrell, Molly's great hunting friend. The Burrell family were great 'Crawley and Horsham' supporters. (They still own a great sporting estate, and Mark is a joint Master of the 'Crawley and Horsham').

When Molly retired from hunting, her Mastership ended, on 29th April, 1961. During the eighty-four days' hunting of her final season, forty brace of foxes were killed, with a pack of twenty-two-and-a-half couple hounds.

Retirement, however, did not end her interest in the hunt. She continued to ride until arthritis forced her to give up. Even then, she went on attending meets and various shows, in her Land-Rover, and breeding the hounds.

Appendix B

Charles' Hunting Journals

Charles started his Hunting Journals in the 1925-26 season, when he was scarcely seven years old. First riding with the Surrey Union, he mentions he was blooded for the third time on 8th September.

Some of the early journal entries are printed in a childish hand but he was ably assisted and encouraged by his mother, who also made entries for him. By 1928, he was writing more freely and from then on, made all his own entries.

His first favourite ponies were Kate and Kitty. He rode them over forty times with the Surrey Union. In 1929, he had a new pony called Vermouth and about that time he was riding regularly with the Crawley and Horsham hounds.

In January, 1931, he rode out alone for the first time. Soon afterwards, he was riding his mother's own horses, including Champagne, Blackie, Captive Balloon, Brown Mare, Diamond Queen, Standfast, and Gold Flake.

During those early days, the meets he attended were mostly local ones, at Ellens Green, Walliswood, Romanswood, Northlands, Kingsfold, Lions Corner, Rowhook and Ockley. There were many times when classes 'interfered' with his hunting activities, but he was drawn back to the sport at every opportunity.

Altogether, he rode to hounds one hundred and seventy times over a period of fifteen years. Then he went off to war, but still maintaining his interest in the hunt. He managed a couple of days' hunting jackal in North Africa, riding Arab ponies. He sent records of this to his mother, to be entered in his journal.

Appendix C

Game Book Entries

One sporting activity enjoyed by all the Gregsons was a walk round the estate with gun and dogs. Then of course there were the seasonal shoots with family and friends, when local men and boys would be employed to drive the woods and fields.

Rabbits were at pest proportions throughout the country before the advent of myxomatosis, and the numbers needed to be decreased at every opportunity.

Records were kept in a Game Book, not only of numbers shot but where, those present, weather conditions and time of year. Individuals at shoots generally had their own Game Book, and a number are retained in the family.

Major George Mackay, with his grandson, Roger Mann

One of the earliest Game Books kept is that of Molly's father, George Mackay, dated 1897. Living at that time at Kington Langley, his record for September of that year reads: 3 pigeons, 1 landrail, 271 partridges, 4 pheasants, 55 hares, and 19 rabbits.

George Mackay was still enjoying a day out with the gun in the 1920's joining the shoots at Ends Place and in other parts of Sussex. Inserted in his Game Book are two interesting old recipes. One is for the curing of mange in dogs, the other involved the sprinkling every day of a few drops of assafetida round the partridge nest, to kill the scent in the event of predators.

Molly records a good month's bag on the estate during November, 1930: 259 pheasants, 2 partridge, 2 woodcock, 56 wildfowl, 16 hares, 48 rabbits, and 8 other varieties. In three days of October, 1938, she records 61 pheasants, 35 partridge, 1 duck, 11 hares and 10 rabbits. Great credit for such good results would have been due to Mr. Trask, the gamekeeper at that time,

Charles, like his mother, was a stickler for keeping records. His Game Book is more detailed that anyone else's in the family. From 1929, when he was ten, he was always accompanied by Mr. Trask, who no doubt offered advice on safety, and instructed him in the use of shotguns. Charles mentions a proud moment in 1930, when Mr. Trask allowed him to use his twelve-bore gun and he successfully shot two rabbits with one cartridge.

Although most of the family's bags consisted of rabbits, it is interesting to note that, at various times, it also included pigeons, duck, hares, woodcock, teal, snipe, widgeon, and geese, some of which are rarely sighted today.

When in Scotland for the grouse and salmon season (with H.G.G., 1935-36, on leave from India) the birds they shot included 3 curlew, 7 plovers, and 8 golden plovers. While out with friends during August and September, 1,958 grouse were shot.

Charles notes that by 1935, both his own and Geoffrey's shooting had greatly improved. Geoffrey's gun was a .410 bore. The book records that David O'Cock was rather dangerous, and their grandpa shot a mistlethrush in mistake for a pigeon!

Their regular walk round the estate to shoot rabbits had a second, essential importance, for the rabbits provided regular food for the ferrets which gave them some great days' shooting and netting.

The last entries in Charles' Game Book were in 1939, before he went to war, except for the entry sent home to his mother to record.

Below are names of many members of the family and friends who, at various times, enjoyed the shoots between 1925 and 1938.

Grandpa Mackay	Sir M. Burrell
Harry	Lord Lawrence
Molly	Lord Denbigh
Charles	Lady Bailey
Geoffrey	Colonel Wicks
Peggy (Harry's sister)	Colonel de-Gray
Guy Tylden-Wright	Colonel Marks
R.G. Ireland	Major Reynolds
Gordon Lucas	Major Neilson
K. Scott	H.G.M. Gendstone
G.N. Dickens	John McKergow
H. Stokes	G.N. Stocker
M. Tatts Baines	J. Newman
J. Eden	Revd. Matthews
R. Tinsley	Revd. E.L. Brown
J. Jarvis	Revd. Harvey
J. Spencer	H.G. Latilla
F.S. Horn	F.R. Brown

Appendix D

Molly's Gift to the Tate Gallery

It was Molly's wish that, following her death, three paintings should be presented to the Tate Gallery. These paintings are now on view in the British Sporting Art Trust/Vestey Gallery at the National Horse-racing Museum, Newmarket.

87.10. *Returning Home: Crawley and Horsham.*
Lionel Edwards. Oil on canvas. 19 x 28 in. S + D 1960

These three paintings were bequeathed to the Trust by Mrs. H. G. Gregson, who was Master of the Crawley and Horsham for three periods, 1939 to 1948, 1951 to 1958 and 1960 to 1961. Between 1948-1951 she was joint master with Lt. Col. H. Green and acted for the committee between 1958-1960, a stretch of 22 years.

Lionel Edwards needs no introduction to members of the Trust. Details of his life and work were presented in the illustrated catalogue that accompanied the B.S.A.T. Exhibition of 1986 (copies available, price £5.00, from the secretary). The three paintings are interesting in that they cover a span of 27 years. The 1933 oil was made when Edwards was at the height of his powers. Under the winter sky, near Partridge Green, the South Downs stretch away to the north in a distant panorama. The field wait expectantly behind the commanding figure of the Master Lt. Col. the Hon. C. G. Cubitt, D.S.O., as the huntsmen Charles Denton blowing his horn, takes the hounds to a holloa, the whipper-in, on the left of the picture, cracks his whip to encourage the stragglers. Waiting with the Master are Col. McKergow and Maj. Riley.

The water colour of 1947 brings to us the bright

sunlight of a spring morning as the pack leave Chanctonbury Ring. The huntsman is still Charles Denton and the whipper-in, with the hounds, is Reg Hirons. By this time Edwards had abandoned the fluent style of gouache that he mastered between the wars and was using water colour strengthened with only an occasional stroke of body colour.

The retirement presentation picture of 1960 shows the whipper-in Reg Hirons stopping hounds at Twineham Church. Following on is the huntsman Jack Clarke. An appropriate comment on the end of 22 mastership. Although a competent study, the earlier magic of landscape and sky has with age and failing sight disappeared.

This brings to seven the number of paintings by Lionel Edwards in the Trust's collection.

Appendix E

Cricket match as reported in the *Sussex Guardian,* about 1928-1930

Warnham v Mr. H. Gregson's Eleven

A very enjoyable match was played on the Warnham ground on Monday, when a side organised by Mr. Gregson, owing to the absence of her husband who is in India, played at the Warnham Club. The teams were entertained to lunch and tea by Mrs. Gregson at the Sussex Oak. Warnham were winners. Batting first, the village club scored 70 for the first wicket and had compiled 215 for the whole side. Their opponents were dismissed for 78.

Warnham

G N Dickins	c Tinsley	b Ireland	33
E Charman	lbw	b Graham	40
R Booth		b Stubbs	19
F Edwards			69
H Charman	c & b	Spencer	1
J Woodall		b Tanner	4
S Booth	c Ireland	b Tanner	0
Revd. F S Farebrother*	c Grenville-Grey	b Tanner	1
J Stanford		b Eden	5
F Tarrant*		b Eden	3
E Muggeridge	not out		2
		Extras	38
			215

---

* *Later Revd. Canon Tarrant*

Mr. Gregson's Eleven

G B Eden		b Muggeridge	27
E J Tanner		b Stanford	2
C Grenville-Grey	c Farebrother	b Muggeridge	17
K Stubbs		b Stanford	9
G L Graham	lbw	b Muggeridge	4
R L Tinsley		b Muggeridge	14
J Spencer		b Stanford	4
S S Oxley	not out		0
A G Puttick		b Muggeridge	0
		Extras	1
			78

Appendix F

Staff Reminiscences

This next, major Appendix is concerned with the staff at Ends Place, and with personal reminiscences of their employer.

As long-serving members of the indoor staff, Joyce Mary Driver and Marjorie Leslie knew their mistress well.

Joyce Driver first joined the staff at Ends Place in 1953. At that time, her stepfather was head cowman. Her early duties were as general live-in help and she then earned an annual wage of £81. Some years later, this was raised to £2.5s.0d. a week. She worked from 9am to 2pm, then from 7pm to 9pm.

To supplement her wages, Joyce also worked a few hours at Strood Park. When Molly heard about this, she had her sacked from that job, so that she could concentrate on her employment at Ends Place.

Strood Park
(now Farlington School)

Marjorie Leslie and her son, William, then aged three, joined the staff in 1973, to live in and help as and where needed. Mrs. Gregson became devoted to William and he, to her. Marjorie later moved to a house in Tillets Lane.

Joyce and Marjorie decided to combine their accounts of life with Mrs. Gregson at Ends Place...

Joyce and Marjorie's story

Joyce and Marjorie talked about how poorly paid they were. Some idea of this can be gleaned from the general scale of wages (already mentioned in earlier pages of this book) before World War II. They went on to say that the low wages were in fact greatly compensated for, by the provision of excellent food. Wages were much improved after the war.

Work in the house was not arduous but the working week was "much too long". They had one day a week off, but Sunday was always a working day.

Mrs. Gregson was not a demanding employer but she liked to have her staff round her at all times. She had an amazing knack of making them delighted to do anything for her, even though a few minutes before they may have been "grumbling like mad at the prospect!" They were always treated with the unfailing courtesy she showed to everyone, from the Duke of Beaufort to the local dustman.

Mrs. Gregson never came to terms with decimalisation, and always insisted on being told the prices of the things in "proper money".

She had an incredibly sweet tooth, always enjoying "lashings of sugar", syrup or jam, and she loved chocolate. When she developed diabetes, it showed what an iron will she had, for she managed to control this craving for sweet things. She allowed herself one diabetic chocolate a day and she allowed the dogs one each, too (diabetic or not!). She shared all her meals with the dogs.

Her strong will and great courage also showed during her constant battle with the terrible pain of arthritis. Never really complaining, whenever asked how she was she would reply "not too bad".

It was a tragedy when she became more or less housebound. She found it increasingly difficult, at times impossible, to make the supreme effort needed to drag herself from her wheelchair into the Land-Rover, so that she could go to see her beloved horses. She would also go to the local meets, which required "psyching herself up" for hours beforehand.

Both Joyce and Marjorie had no hesitation in saying that she was "a real lady", and had the most profound effect on their lives by *being herself.*

Her capabilities as a vehicle driver, in her late years driving the Land-Rover, were almost legendary.

Until Marjorie and William joined the household, Mrs. Gregson had slept alone in the house for quite some time. She always had her shotgun close at hand as a safety precaution.

She was known to keep a careful watch from her bedroom window, and it was during one of these checks at night that she saw a fluttering of clothes outside. After making the customary challenge: "Stand and deliver", without getting a reply, she fired. In the morning, a staff apron was found on the washing line, riddled with pellets, once again proving her ability as a fine shot...

Joyce and Marjorie would always remember the earlier,

happy days when, with the house full of guests, grand luncheon and dinner parties were held, during the South of England Show, at Ardingly, and the Crawley and Horsham Hunt Show. The huge dining table would be laid with beautiful silver and crystal glasses.

During their time at Ends Place, one of the cooks was Annie Huff, and Mrs. Gregson named a racehorse after her. The mare never went into training but she won countless Championship Classes, when sold as a large hack, under the name of Black Gold.

They frequently referred to Mrs. Gregson's keen interest in her horses, bred for racing, hunting and as show farm horses. She also showed prize-winning cattle. Her interest was well-known throughout the country with regard to all her animals, particularly her hounds. She was seldom seen without her favourite retrievers and terriers when out walking. In her chair at home, a cat would often be on her lap and terriers, at her feet.

Joyce and Marjorie named some of the dogs best remembered in the house and kennel:

Prim	*in house*	Badger	*in house and kennel*
Lou	*in house*	Judy	*in kennel*
Quaint	*in house*	Patsy	*in kennel*
Becky Sharp	*in house*	Cumper	*in kennel*

Odd names, perhaps, but then Mrs. Gregson often used pet names. A particular one she had for George Tusler, her groom, was 'Georgie Porgie'.

Another member of staff they remembered was Bill Pearce, head cowman, who lived with his wife in what was formerly the groom's cottage at the stables. His wife, René, was employed in the house as a domestic. Bill Pearce was "an awful man who could not get staff to stay with him".

Joyce and Marjorie mentioned two gardeners: Mr. Gumbrill, who cycled the five miles from Roffey, near Horsham, and his successor, Reg Palmer, who cycled four miles from Barns Green. Reg they always remember as the gardener who kept the lawns round the house beautifully cut but seldom cleared away the cuttings unless guests were expected, so that there were always "unsightly mounds of mown grass everywhere". Nor was the knotted bailing twine with which he used to separate the lawns from the drive an attractive sight! Riders and walkers using the bridleway tended to ignore these barriers. In a fit of exasperation one day, Reg carried out his long-threatened promise to put up a notice. He could not understand why Marjorie became most hysterical on reading THIS IS NOT A PUBIC RIGHT OF WAY. The notice was hastily taken down, although they think Reg never did quite know what was wrong with it.

On one occasion, the groom, Paul Mort, was long-reining one of Mrs. Gregson's young horses, Chavey Down, past the house, so that she could observe the animal. Unfortunately, Mr. Trask, who had been inspecting something in the hedgerow nearby, chose that moment to appear. This startled the young horse, causing him to prance all over the lawn, which brought a furious Reg "hustling round the corner, threatening to sue the groom!"

No great damage was done but poor Reg - "a dear man but singularly lacking in a sense of humour" - never realised that threatening to sue Paul Mort for allowing Mrs. Gregson's horse to cavort over Mrs. Gregson's lawn was hardly the right thing to do. Even less did he appreciate everyone else finding the episode so amusing - "even the horse!"

Joyce's and Marjorie's days are still filled with Ends

Place memories. Little things stick in their minds, like the time when large numbers of bees invaded the study. At one time, jackdaws were a nuisance in the chimneys.

Like many people, they believed that such days will never return. They think that when Mrs Gregson died, a whole way of life died with her. Even so, never a day passes without their still using one or another of her fascinating expressions.

Mr Jack Foran
Groom at Ends Place for nearly 40 years

Jack Foran, originally from Navan, Co. Meath, Ireland, came to England in 1906 and for a time worked for Mr. Robinson, a racehorse trainer at Beckhampton, Wiltshire. There, he had charge of the well known Derby horse, Crachenor.

He served as groom to Harry Gregson before World War 1. After that war, he and his wife, Kate, had "The Bear" Public House in Devizes, Wiltshire. In 1920, he learned that Mr. Harry Gregson had placed an advertisement in the local newspaper, asking for news of Jack's whereabouts.

Jack contacted him, and was offered the post of groom at Ends Place, which he accepted. He and his wife, with their young son, John, moved to the cottage in the stable block at the rear of the main house. Jack continued to work for the Gregsons until his retirement in 1958. His successor was George Tusler, who had worked under him from 1930 to 1939. His family then moved to the cottage he had bought, at 40, Friday Street, Warnham. He died in 1964.

His son, known as Johnny, also worked for the Gregsons, as an assistant groom to his father, and he still lives in the village. He recalls that there were times when Mrs. Gregson went to Kington Langley, hunting, and his father would also go, to look after the horses.

Sometimes, Jack would be instructed to take horses to Tilbury Docks, to be shipped to India - part of a regular two-way shipment of bloodstock between Ends Place and the Calcutta Estate Stables.

He remembered many of the horses at Ends Place. Charles, he said, had a beautiful horse named Sidney, which he regularly rode to hunts and successfully rode to win a Point-to-Point at Cambridge. There is a Plumpton race called The Clapper Cup, for which the Gregsons gave the trophy.

Among the best of the thoroughbreds was Moretons, a top class, two-mile chaser, who won twenty-eight races. Another was Dormant, who once beat the famous Arkle, and won the King George V Stakes at Kempton Park and the Whitbread Cup at Sandown Park.

Two other great 'chasers were Border Ranger (1927-30) and Overseas, winner of County Hurdles (1937-40). The latter was killed at Cheltenham, over fences when ridden by John Hislop, to whom he was given on the outbreak of war.

One reflection which brings a smile to John's face is that of a character horse called Clapper (after which the Plumpton Trophy was named). He was impossible to train for the flat but proved to be and excellent 'chaser and won many races.

The Trask Family

The Trask family lived on the estate for seventy years.

Alfred Trask was Head Gamekeeper at Ends Place for almost fifty years. He died in 1976, aged 88.

Mr. Trask moved to Warnham in 1927 and live with his wife and daughter, Muriel, in a tied house at the bottom of Tillets Lane. Muriel remembered that the rent of the house was six shillings per week but cannot recall what her father's wages were then. Those were the days when children were "seen and not heard".

Mr. Trask's duties entailed the rearing of pheasants, partridges and ducks, in preparation for the annual winter shoots. The young birds were reared in the orchard behind their house, with protection against predators. Muriel loved that time of year, for she was permitted to feed the birds. When large enough, they were transferred to an adjoining field, later to be released in the woods.

Rearing birds was only one of the endless jobs that gamekeepers were required to do. The general condition of the estate was Mr. Trask's responsibility. He had to note which ditches, gates, fencing and hedges required attention. He had to make sure that gates were closed, and keep an eye open for poachers.

Mr. Trask would have been doing the

Alfred Trask and his Retriever   same job for about

twelve years when war was declared, and his way of life dramatically changed. His main task then became the supervision of the production of more food on the estate. He also took control of livestock, discussing with Mrs. Gregson which fields to plough and what to plant. Hay-making and harvest time kept him very busy.

Most of the hay and corn was stored at Chalkridge Farm, in Byfleets Lane, and was threshed annually on that site. Many livestock were also housed at that farm. The manager at Chalkridge during a later period was Mr. Marshall.

Strood Farm was where the milking was done and it also had a hayloft for storage.

Muriel Trask told me that her father kept a meticulous record of all his work at Ends Place although, regrettably, this record appears to have been lost.

She enjoyed her years in Warnham. She was educated at the local school, played in the stool ball team, attended folk dances, ballroom dances and the very popular whist drives, all held in the old village hall. At home, she enjoyed playing whist, cribbage and draughts with her family and friends.

On 14th November, 1944, in St. Margaret's Church, Warnham, she married Harold Dann, whom she had met when she was in the W.A.A.F. Harold was in the R.A.F. for four and a half years, serving in the Far East. Muriel died in 1991.

Mr. George Tusler

George Tusler was seventeen years of age when he first joined the Gregson staff. Put to work under Mr. Foran, the head groom, he was very happy at his work and loved the horses.

In 1933, he married and went to live at South Lodge, later moving into North Lodge. Following Mr. Foran's retirement, George took over the stud groom's job.

When first employed by Mrs. Gregson, George's wage was £1 per week. On marriage, he received £2 per week, with free accommodation in the bungalow. His promotion to stud groom increased his wage to £7 per week. When he retired at sixty-five, he was receiving £14 per week

George remembered the Marden family living in Hill House, and a Mr. and Mrs. Marquest living in the Tin Bungalow. The last family to occupy the Tin Bungalow were the Capons. Albert George Capon died on 15th December, 1989, and is buried close to Molly Gregson in Warnham churchyard. He was predeceased by his wife, Annie Caroline, who died on 11th October, 1973.

George was an employee of Mrs. Gregson's for forty-eight years. He died in 1990.

Mrs. Doris Downer

Doris Downer, née Belton, was born in Broadridge Heath in 1902.

Her parents emigrated to America in the early 1900s, fully intending to take Doris with them. Unfortunately, she developed measles just before the sailing date and, in consequence, was not allowed to board ship. She was left behind, in the care of Mr. and Mrs. Marden, who lived at Hill House Farm. She took their name.

George and Kate Marden were tenant farmers at Hill House. The small farm had a variety of animals. They dispensed milk and other farm products in the village, by horse and trap.

Doris has happy memories of Hill House.

The previous occupant had been Major Ince, recorded in the Warnham Census as being resident there from 1905 to 1909.

Doris remembers that carved in the stonework over the dining-room fireplace was the date 1578, confirming that the house was of medieval construction. She also remembers stained glass in an upstairs window, commemorating a visit by Queen Elizabeth I.

Doris's husband, 'Nobby' Downer, was one of the early stewards Warnham Comrades Club.

After a time in hospital, Doris is now back at home, still looking after herself, cooking, and gardening - at 92.

Her daughter, Mrs. Nora Ann Goodrich, is also still resident in the village, and very much helped with the provision of this memoir.

Appendix G

Names of Staff, with residence where known
(not in order of service)

Farm Managers
Walter Payne, Bailiff/Manager to Charles Bulpin Gregson
Mr. Arthur Marshall, Farm Manager for Molly Gregson

Gardeners, with other duties

Frank Cox	Friday Street
Harry Webb, Head gardener (kitchen)	Tin Bungalow
Alfred Munday, Head gardener	Lodge
Fred Webb	Pump House
Fred Hetherington	Church Street
Jock Christensen	Bell Road
Mr. Scott (Senior)	Bell Road
Ted Scott	Bell Road
Jack Teach	Tin Bungalow
Reg Palmer	Burns Green
C Gumbrill	Roffy

Grooms

Mr J. Bowers, Head groom	
Mr G. Tusler, Head groom	
Mr J. Foran, Head groom	Stable Cottage
John Foran (son), assistant to father	Stable Cottage
Paul Mort, Groom	

Grooms were required to wear leather belts with reflectors

Chauffeurs
Mr. Padwick ('Paddy')   Cottage (rear of
                                         house
Mr. Tuggles (1916)   House opposite
                                         Front Lodge

Cowmen
Albert Cox
Harry Stocker, Head cowman
Tom Stock
Bob Marshall
Jack Marshall (son)
Mr. Robson, Head cowman
Dave J. Robson (son - killed in 1939-45 war, trooper,
        Royal Armoured Corps)
Bill Pearce, Head cowman
James Pace

Carters
Steven Farley   Friday Street
Eric Linfield (senior)
Fred Linfield
Tom Nightingale
George Tilbury
Mr. Carver, Senior ploughman   Newmans Cottage

Farm Workers
Ben Longridge, former Manager,
Lower Lodge Farm, Fernhurst
(present when Mrs. Gregson died)   Stable Cottage

Mr. Marshall, Manager   Chalkridge Farm
Mr. Robinson, Foreman
Tom Yates, Tractor driver   Newmans Cottage

Bert Farnes
Charlie Davey
Charlie Francis   Friday Street
Paddy Doyle   Strood Lodge
Frank Cox
Charlie Hillman (Dewey)   Geerings Cottage
Jack Capon   Tin Bungalow
Mr. Luffman
Mr. Tilbury
Mr. Short   Friday Street
Jack Higgins
Mr. Simmonds   Front Lodge
Mr. Hillman

Woodmen
Jack Nightingale   Cokelers Cottage
Geoffrey Payne   Friday Street

General Help
Mrs. Marjorie Leslie   Lived in
Mrs. Joyce Mary Driver, and   Lived in
Mrs. Grace Jones   Lived in
(both present when Mrs. Gregson died)

Household Staff

Mrs. Mumford
Housekeeper brought from the
London residence during hunting
season, pre World War II   Lived in

General
Mrs. Conibear   Tillets Lanes

Mrs. Carver
Mrs. Padwick

Cottage (rear of house)

Mrs. Alexander	General, stores, etc.	
Rose Muggeridge	Maid	Lived in
Muriel Nightingale	Maid	Friday Street
Rose Musgrave (née Street)	Maid	Lived in
Mr. Booker	Odd job man	Church Street
Rich Linfield	Odd job man	

Senior House Staff

Mr. Alexander	Butler	
Mr. Clark	Butler	
Mr. Simmonds	Butler	
Mr. Bishop	Under-butler	
Fred Godley	Under-butler (Warnham Footballer)	
Mr. Harper	Last butler to serve the house	Front Lodge (walked to work down front drive)
Mr. R. Linfield		

Nannies

Muriel Muggeridge	to Harry	Friday Street
Miss Wade (Always known as "Miss", even by M.G.)	to Charles and Geoffrey	Lived in
Mrs. Gox	Governess (Crammer to Charles and Geoffrey)	

Numerous other Governesses were employed but none ever lasted long! Charles and Geoffrey preferred the company of Gamekeepers Trask and Lion, and the stable staff

Gamekeepers

Mr. Fred Lion	Cottage (rear of house)
Mr. John Lion	
Mr. Alfred Trask	Tillets Lane
Mr. Bill Baker	Pump House

Bailiff

Mr. Bill Baker	Pump House

Secretary

Peggy Bannister	Secretary to H.G Gregson

Horses

Mr. Jack Foran	In charge when horses were
Mr. Matthews	transported by rail. Also drove the second horsebox they had made by Vincents of Reading. (Their first was the earliest made by that company in 1928.)

Companions

Gladys Eyken	At girls' school with M.G., and her constant, lifelong companion
Joyce Gerard	In attendance on Mrs. Gregson in her later years

Appendix H

Family, friends and associates

Mr. O'Cock

He was always known as 'Oco'. While working in Harry Gregson's office in Calcutta, he met and married Peggy Gregson.

Their sons, David and Michael, were at Harrow with Charles and Geoffrey. Michael later became a Brigadier in the Irish Guards.

Guy Tilden-Wright

Peggy's second husband, he was often seen doing aerobatics over the village and estate, in his plane. He crashed in the sand field behind Ends Place. Their daughter, Diana, married Captain Fawcus, of the Irish Guards.

Sir Newton and Lady Moore

Resident at Mayes Park, Warnham, they and their children were great friends of the family, Their daughter, Mollie, was a great friend of Charles'. They hoped to marry after the war.

Mr. Tatts Baines of Westbrook Hall, and
Mr. George Dickens of Rowhook Manor

These two very keen cricketers were always in the Estate team. Mr. Dickens was known as "Stonewall Dickens", for the long periods he spent at the crease, and for slow scoring.

EPILOGUE

Ends Place has risen from the rubble, even larger than before, as Warnham Manor - on the same foundations but a few yards to the east. The front door now faces west, to avoid the cool northern aspect so beloved by C.B. Gregson.

In the grounds, the twin Sussex oaks, planted by "Mr. Charles" to commemorate with his wife Anne the building of their English home, still stand, proud and strong. The pond from which the swans once flew, on C.B.'s purchase and valuation, is clear of bullrushes again and stocked with trout. The rose garden where Charles and I buried the family silver in 1939, has been levelled and is back in lawn.

On Tillets Lane, planning permission has been granted for 'starter' homes for Warnham people and Ends Place employees, in the Rainbow Field, as Molly wanted.

In Warnham village, the roof of St. Margaret's Church is being repaired. The War Memorial surround is clean and tidy, with no sweet papers (which so worried Molly) and the church wall has been repaired.

Molly's headstone faces the park at Warnham Court, where the dairy cows of Tommy Luckin - her former farming partner at Ends Place - now graze.

May she rest in peace.

G.G.A.G.
December, 1993

The Hunter's Requiem

Lay me to rest by the grand old yew
Close by the Churchyard wall
In my scarlet coat with my hands on my breast
Waiting the last great call.

Let no stone mark my narrow bed
Only the soft green sod
And the sombre pall of yew overhead
Guarding the Church of God.

So let me wait to the last great Trump.
O'er valley and hill shall sound
When my master shall summon the final meet
Of riders and horse and hound.

And I fancy when all flesh is gathered in
There will come from the moor and the glen
The Fox and the Badger, the Horse and the Dog,
As well as the sons of men.

We shall clear our last fence on that wonderful day
Ride strong in the name of the blest.
But the sinless creatures of woodland and lea
Will be miles ahead of the rest.

'Croucher'

This poem was much loved by Molly Gregson, and was found among her papers.

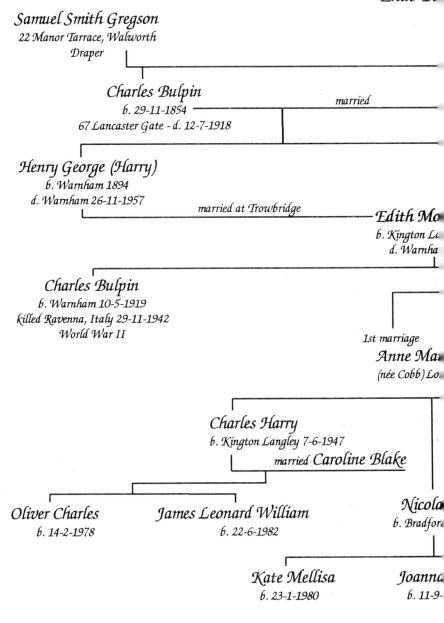

Samuel Smith Gregson
22 Manor Tarrace, Walworth
Draper

Charles Bulpin
b. 29-11-1854
67 Lancaster Gate - d. 12-7-1918

married

Henry George (Harry)
b. Warnham 1894
d. Warnham 26-11-1957

married at Trowbridge

Edith Mo
b. Kington L
d. Warnha

Charles Bulpin
b. Warnham 10-5-1919
killed Ravenna, Italy 29-11-1942
World War II

1st marriage
Anne Ma
(née Cobb) Lo

Charles Harry
b. Kington Langley 7-6-1947
married Caroline Blake

Oliver Charles
b. 14-2-1978

James Leonard William
b. 22-6-1982

Nicola
b. Bradfor

Kate Mellisa
b. 23-1-1980

Joanna
b. 11-9-